Your Horoscope 2023

....

Aquarius

21 January – 19 February

igloobooks

igloobooks

Published in 2022
First published in the UK by Igloo Books Ltd
An imprint of Igloo Books Ltd
Cottage Farm, NN6 0BJ, UK
Owned by Bonnier Books
Sveavägen 56, Stockholm, Sweden
www.igloobooks.com

0722 001
2 4 6 8 10 9 7 5 3 1
ISBN 978-1-80108-397-3

Written by Sally Kirkman
Additional content by Belinda Campbell and Denise Evans
Designed by Richard Sykes
Edited by Katie Taylor

Printed and manufactured in China

INTRODUCTION

. . . .

This 15-month guide has been designed and written to give a concise and accessible insight into both the nature of your star sign and the year ahead. Divided into two main sections, the first section of this guide will give you an overview of your character in order to help you understand how you think, perceive the world and interact with others and – perhaps just as importantly – why. You'll soon see that your zodiac sign is not just affected by a few stars in the sky, but by planets, elements, and a whole host of other factors, too.

The second section of this guide is made up of daily forecasts. Use these to increase your awareness of what might appear on your horizon so that you're better equipped to deal with the days ahead. While this should never be used to dictate your life, it can be useful to see how your energies might be affected or influenced, which in turn can help you prepare for what life might throw your way.

By the end of these 15 months, these two sections should have given you a deeper understanding and awareness of yourself and, in turn, the world around you. There are never any definite certainties, but with an open mind you will find guidance for what might be, and learn to take more control of your own destiny.

THE CHARACTER OF THE WATER BEARER

. . . .

A rebel in the style of James Dean, with or without a cause, Aquarius is the Water Bearer sign of the zodiac that is here to give to their communities whilst also making waves. With the rebellious songs of the sixties in their ear, breaking tradition and challenging conventions is what this free-thinking air sign is all about. Whilst the songs of the 1960s might lay claim to the age of Aquarius, no one can quite agree on when this sign's astrological age begins or ends. An astrological age is thought to be close to 2000 years long and defined by the associated sign, so why is the age of Aquarius the one that everyone makes a song and dance about? Belonging to the eleventh house in the zodiac calendar that represents community and friendship, Aquarians and their astrological age are sure to influence and change up the whole world and everyone in it as this sign is about realising common goals, hopes and dreams for the future.

Co-ruled by rule-abiding Saturn and rebellious Uranus, Aquarians can be unapologetic when it comes to breaking tradition and will march to the beat of their own drum alone if they must, whether that's to the reggae beat of Bob Marley or the classical compositions of Mozart. Born in the middle of winter, fixed Aquarians may be set in their way of thinking, rightly or wrongly. With a positive energy, Aquarians can be wonderful at acting on what they believe. Aquarian activists Rosa Parks with her Montgomery Bus Boycott and Yoko Ono with her bed-ins for peace show how this sign can act against injustices. Aquarians are known for being progressive thinkers, with an eye fixed firmly on the future, which is perhaps why technological advancements are often closely linked with this futuristic sign. With Aquarians' devotion to their social responsibility and the speed at which technology is sky-rocketing, the age of Aquarius may well be in full swing as social media activism, or hashtivism, for example in movements like #TimesUp which continue to gather followers globally. With influential philanthropists and activists like Aquarians Eddie Izzard and Oprah Winfrey belonging to this star sign, the voice of Aquarius is sure to be heard for decades to come.

THE WATER BEARER

Despite being an air sign, it is the giving Water Bearer that symbolises Aquarius. Ruled by Saturn, who was named after the Roman god of agriculture, Aquarius' symbol of the Water Bearer shows the eternal current of positive energy that flows from this sign and helps the world to grow. The gifts of the Water Bearer can be numerous, but this air sign is likely to influence society most substantially through their progressive thoughts and ideas. Aquarians can be visionaries, and this air sign's alternative way of thinking combined with their outgoing nature means that others are likely to listen to what they have to say. Although not everyone may agree with the rebel-minded Aquarius, this futuristic thinker is usually ahead of their time, their symbol of the Water Bearer suggests that what this sign will bring to the world will be given with the best of intentions for the goal of a brighter future.

SATURN AND URANUS

The second largest planet in the solar system, Saturn stands out as loud and proud as its co-ruled sign Aquarius. Belonging to the eleventh house of community, this Saturn-ruled sign will likely take their social responsibility extremely seriously and may focus all their hard work into building a community that they believe to be just and fair. With the authority of Saturn co-guiding this sign, their fixed way of thinking can at times come across as a little preachy or superior, so this air sign should try to always listen and remain open-minded. Co-ruled by radical Uranus, Aquarians may be all about change and liberation from the rules of Saturn. Uranus is known for its off-kilter axis which could go a long way to explaining the alternative and unconventional traits that some Aquarians can display. Saturn's size and Uranus' unique tilt make these two planets stand out in the solar system and could act as a reminder to all belonging to this extraordinary sign that Aquarians were born to be a little different.

ELEMENTS, MODES AND POLARITIES

Each sign is made up of a unique combination of three defining groups: elements, modes and polarities. Each of these defining parts can manifest themselves in good and bad ways and none should be seen as a positive or a negative – including the polarities! Just like a jigsaw puzzle, piecing these groups together can help illuminate why each sign has certain characteristics and help us find a balance.

ELEMENTS

Fire: Dynamic and adventurous, signs with fire in them can be extroverted. Others are naturally drawn to them because of the positive light they give off, as well as their high levels of energy and confidence.

Earth: Signs with the earth element are steady and driven with their ambitions. They make for a solid friend, parent or partner due to their grounded influence and nurturing nature.

Air: The invisible element that influences each of the other elements significantly, air signs will provide much-needed perspective to others with their fair thinking, verbal skills and key ideas.

Water: Warm in the shallows and freezing as ice. This mysterious element is essential to the growth of everything around it, through its emotional depth and empathy.

MODES

Cardinal: Pioneers of the calendar, cardinal signs jump-start each season and are the energetic go-getters.

Fixed: Marking the middle of the calendar, fixed signs firmly denote and value steadiness and reliability.

Mutable: As the seasons end, the mutable signs adapt and give themselves over gladly to the promise of change.

POLARITIES

Positive: Typically extroverted, positive signs take physical action and embrace outside stimulus in their life.

Negative: Usually introverted, negative signs value emotional development and experiencing life from the inside out.

AQUARIUS IN BRIEF

The table below shows the key attributes of Aquarians. Use it for quick reference and to understand more about this fascinating sign.

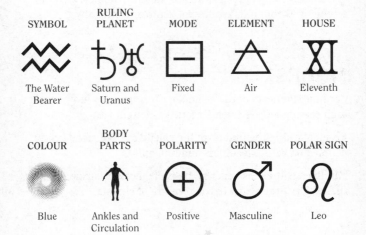

SYMBOL	RULING PLANET	MODE	ELEMENT	HOUSE
The Water Bearer	Saturn and Uranus	Fixed	Air	Eleventh

COLOUR	BODY PARTS	POLARITY	GENDER	POLAR SIGN
Blue	Ankles and Circulation	Positive	Masculine	Leo

ROMANTIC RELATIONSHIPS

. . . .

Aquarians can be some of the friendliest and most alluring of all people and are unlikely to be short of admirers. They may have a laid-back approach to finding a partner, and if they are in a relationship can even seem aloof, but devotion is usually steadfast with this fixed sign. If an Aquarian is not overly emotional with their partner and is much happier to exchange thoughts and ideas than feelings, it is not necessarily because they are not emotionally invested in the relationship. A closed-off Aquarius could struggle with a water sign partner and likewise, water signs might not warm to the cool exterior of this air sign. Warm and passionate fire signs are sure to raise this air sign's temperature and as these elements share a positive outgoing energy, plenty of common interests could be shared. As is the case with many air signs, their love can feel like a trip to the heavens or a painful plummet to Earth. But even if this sign falls out of love, the friendships that they form can be so firm that they can withstand a break-up and be the rule breakers that do in fact stay friends with their exes.

Whilst being highly independent, Aquarians are all about teamwork so can truly thrive in a loving relationship so long as it stems from a firm friendship and mutual beliefs. This giving Water Bearer sign may struggle to give up their prized individualism in exchange for a partnership, and their fixed attitude can give them a stubborn edge that makes them resistant to accepting any dramatic changes to their lifestyle. A partner that understands their Aquarian's desire to remain autonomous and is fully accepting of their uniqueness is one that this sign should try and hold on to. A jealous or possessive lover is a big no-no for this free spirit. Aquarians who want to let love into their lives should understand that change is inevitable and what can feel like an upheaval to their independence is more of a loving revolution.

ARIES: COMPATIBILITY 3/5

Two signs known for their admirable quality of being a good friend to all, Aries and Aquarius should have a good solid foundation of friendship to base their romantic relationship on. This coupling of air and fire will always make for a fuelled love. Independence is key for keeping your Aquarius lover happy, so Aries should be careful with trying to control the relationship or forcing Aquarius to commit too soon. Whilst these two signs have many things in common, it will be discovering each other's differences that will be essential in keeping both partners interested in this relationship.

TAURUS: COMPATIBILITY 1/5

Taurus and Aquarius aren't an obvious match on paper – it's unlikely that these two will find each other on a matchmaking website! The core differences between these signs make a romantic spark unlikely but should not be ruled out. Aquarius is partly ruled by the planet Uranus, symbolising rebellion and change, i.e. some Taureans' worst nightmare. For the easy life-seeking Taurus who likes what they know, the travel-lusting Aquarius can be hard to keep up with. However, these two signs are both fixed and have the potential to make each other stronger if they remain open to change.

GEMINI: COMPATIBILITY 4/5

The individualist sign Aquarius and Twin sign Gemini can make for a compatible trio. Born in the eleventh house that signifies community and friendship, Aquarians thrive in groups and will be a fantastic partner to social butterfly Gemini. The mutable nature of Geminis will mean that they are happy to follow their Aquarian fixed lover's lead which will likely bring a steadiness to the relationship. Being both positive and air signs, these two will have plenty in common. With a Gemini's love for change and an Aquarian's need for progress, these two could create a bright and revolutionary future together.

CANCER: COMPATIBILITY 1/5

The rebellious Aquarius and security seeking Cancer are not always an obvious match romantically. Whilst their core character differences may be the cause of arguments, if these two can find common interests that can cement a foundation for friendship then love could still bloom. If Cancer can help intellectual Aquarius give themselves emotionally to a partner, then both could mutually benefit from this unlikely but special meeting of the heart and mind. Find common ground to share and foreign lands to explore and Aquarius and Cancer could find a lasting love together.

LEO: COMPATIBILITY 5/5

Aquarius is the air sign that sparks the embers of Leo's fire element into full blaze. Opposites on the calendar, this combination of shared positive energy, fixed attitudes and complementary elements make Leo and Aquarius two individuals that were astrologically made for each other. These unique characters can be guilty of feeling superior to others so may need to remind themselves to treat each other as their rightful equals. Foremost, this is a friendship sprung from fun and crafted by a shared creativity. The visionary mind of Leo combined with Aquarian ideals could have these two creating a utopic life together.

VIRGO: COMPATIBILITY 2/5

Idealist Aquarius and realist Virgo may not be an obvious match, but this couple can be very happy if they find key ideas and goals to share. The organised Virgo will appreciate the Saturn ruled part of Aquarius that represents structure and order but less so their rebellious Uranus side who enjoys throwing the rulebook out. Airy Aquarius and Mercury-ruled Virgo are both free thinkers and should be good at allowing each other room to breathe in the relationship, which both parties will value in their partner. Optimistic Aquarius and pragmatic Virgo will need to find a shared ambition to balance out their stark differences.

LIBRA: COMPATIBILITY 5/5

When these two air signs of Aquarius and Libra fall in love, it can be a whirlwind romance. Ruled by Venus and Uranus, this may well be a rebellious or radical type of love. Libra is a cardinal sign and is quick to come up with ideas, while an Aquarian's mode is fixed, so makes an ideal partner to actualise their Libra lover's plans. Teamwork really is dreamwork for this outgoing positive couple. The ideals of an Aquarius paired with Libra's righteousness can form a couple that will break down boundaries and create their own rules to make their ideal future.

SCORPIO: COMPATIBILITY 1/5

Mysterious Scorpio and unique Aquarius may well find themselves attracted to one another, but the Scorpion and Water Bearer may need to work hard to keep their relationship off the rocks. Positive Aquarians are outgoing, and socialising in their communities is important. However, this is different for introverted Scorpios, who tend to have a small and intimate circle of friends. Their modes are both fixed, which means they can be resistant to changing their contrasting outlooks. If stable Scorpio can embrace this air sign's free spirited nature and rational Aquarius can provide the intimacy that Scorpio needs, then these two could find their happiness.

SAGITTARIUS: COMPATIBILITY 4/5

Placed two apart on the zodiac calendar, the positive energies of an Aquarian and Sagittarian can be a complementary and exciting love match. The thrilling ideas of a Sagittarius combined with an Aquarian's independent thinking can mean that these stimulating spouses will have plenty to talk about. The fire in Sagittarius brings an enthusiastic energy to the relationship and the fixed mode of Aquarius can help provide a focus to their ideas and bring them into fruition. Communal minded Aquarius and sociable Sagittarius will likely be at the heart of their shared communities and bring great meaning to each other's lives.

CAPRICORN: COMPATIBILITY 1/5

Both ruled by Saturn, Capricorns and Aquarians will usually have a good understanding of the rules of love. However, Aquarians are co-ruled by Uranus, so may rebel against the traditions that most Capricorns value. A Capricorn and an Aquarius can both be extremely independent people, which may be what attracts them to one another, and as a creative couple they can really bring out the best in each other. This is a union of strong personalities and beliefs that may struggle to find common ground due to their opposite negative and positive energies, although their differences and determination could be their success.

AQUARIUS: COMPATIBILITY 3/5

When two air signs fall in love, it is usually a kindred meeting of the minds, but they should remember to share their hearts too. What may have first started as a friendship, the relationship of two Aquarians is unlikely to be stuck in the mud with both parties interested in progressing their feelings further. As a couple they may challenge the norm and their love can certainly seem radical to outsiders. Both individuals can be guilty of being stubborn or superior so should try loosening up their fixed attitudes. If these two share the same vision their future can be thought provoking and innovative.

PISCES: COMPATIBILITY 2/5

Two very giving signs such as Pisces and Aquarius could happily give themselves to each other in love. Whilst an air and water sign may struggle to understand one another, an Aquarian's intellect combined with a Piscean's compassion can form a relationship that speaks to both the heart and head if flexibility and patience is practised by the pair. A fixed and mutable mode can be a complementary match, so long as Aquarians don't try to bend the will of their accommodating Piscean partner. The bond that these two can share when at its best can be sincere and spiritually liberating.

FAMILY AND FRIENDS

. . . .

Having a friend in Aquarius is surely having a friend for life. Whether this faithful sign has seen their chums last week or last year, these friendly souls will happily pick up where they last left off. Despite their likeable positive natures, their original and unconventional thoughts can at times make it hard for this sign to relate to their family and friends. Whether the loved ones of an Aquarius believe in the same things as them or not, surrounding themselves with open-minded people who will listen to their vast and sometimes controversial ideas will help this sign form bonds. Befriending a mutable sign like a Piscean or Sagittarian who will usually welcome a change of perspective could help Aquarians air their ideas freely and without judgment. For an intellectual chat or non-stop gossip, air signs like Libra and Gemini will always be happy to exchange ideas and chat endlessly with their Aquarian friend. Born in the eleventh house of friendship and community, being a member of a club or society is where Aquarians can feel most at home. There can be a secret side to Aquarius, some will certainly value their privacy, so perhaps a secret society or hanging out in a bar off the beaten track will be where to find this sign catching up with friends.

Aquarius' uniqueness could extend to their choice of home as this sign may find that they do not feel comfortable in a traditional setting such as a two-up two-down terraced house. Instead, they may feel more at home in a converted barn or church, or whatever perhaps best suits their one-off personality. Inside an Aquarian's home, their choice of interior is likely to continue to reflect their utterly unique personality; think eclectic and antique trinkets rather than Swedish flat-pack furniture. Wherever this nomadic character decides to settle, building a social network will be key to them and they will no doubt be a positive pillar in their community. Symbolised by the Water Bearer, Aquarians are intent on making their community flourish and their giving and friendly ways will usually have them working in a team for the greater good. This Water Bearer might be found raising money for their local watering hole or at the local council meeting speaking their mind on how to best improve their local area for the benefit of everyone.

When it comes to the family of an Aquarian, they will always try to work as a team. Born in the eleventh house where teamwork is key, Aquarians may be the one that encourages each member of the family to vocalise their thoughts and have a vital input into the way they function as a household. As with their own life, Aquarians may favour an alternative path for their children also. Home schooling may be an Aquarian's preference if they find that their local schools are too traditional for their liking. Aquarians will not want their children to miss out on group activities so enrolling their child in sports or other social clubs could be a priority. However, as with any functional community, the voice of everyone will be heard in an Aquarian's home and their children may have the deciding vote or at least a valid input.

MONEY AND CAREERS

. . . .

Being a certain star sign will not dictate the type of career that you have, although the characteristics that fall under each sign could help you identify the areas in which you could potentially thrive. Conversely, to succeed in the workplace, it is just as important to understand what you are good at as it is to know what you are less brilliant at so that you can see the areas in which you will need to perhaps work harder to achieve your career and financial goals.

When it comes to money, Aquarians are usually far more interested in the exchange of ideas than of cash. If an Aquarian is money focused it will generally be because they want to help their community in some way. To their friends and family, Aquarius is known for their seemingly endless generosity and this Water Bearer will come to parties with their arms full of wine and treats for all. This sign is normally fixated on doing things for the benefit of their fellow human so raising funds for a local charity or donating their money to help restore a nearby youth hostel are the types of projects that this giving sign may like to spend their money on. Aquarians won't typically be satisfied with donating just their money to the good of the community and may find that their vocation is working as a social worker or in another public sector where they believe they can best serve their community and make a difference, like human rights lawyer Amal Clooney, equal rights campaigner Rosa Parks or suffragette Susan B. Anthony. Aquarians want to make their communities better places and make a difference for everyone.

As an air sign, a career that stretches their mind should be well suited to an Aquarian. This futuristic sign could be set on inventing the next world-changing invention, theory or technological advancement like Aquarians Thomas Edison or Charles Darwin. So innovative and outspoken is this sign that people are certainly inclined to listen to them in the workplace, even if their colleagues don't quite agree with their unique perspective. With Saturn by their side, Aquarians will usually be highly devoted to their work responsibilities and can be one of the most reliable and hard-working of signs. The authority given to this sign by Saturn could help Aquarians become a highly successful team manager or commanding boss of their own company, like Duncan Bannatyne. Their positive energy can be a stimulating force in the office, and being born in the eleventh house makes them both inspiring leaders and energetic team players – look at famous Aquarians Abraham Lincoln or Franklin D. Roosevelt to see how this sign can take charge and inspire people even in the trickiest of situations.

Whilst you can't always choose who you work with, it can be advantageous to learn about colleagues' key characteristics through their star signs to try and work out the best ways of working with them. Feeling the influence of radical Uranus can make it hard for Aquarians to follow someone else's rules, so their relationships with managers and bosses could be challenging at times if they do not share the same ethos. Born in the first house that represents the self, Aries could be a colleague that jars with the community-minded Aquarius, whilst fellow air sign Libra could be the pioneering idea-seeking boss that gels well with Aquarius.

HEALTH AND WELLBEING

. . . .

One way in which this air sign can help clear their mind is by making sure that their environment is both peaceful and functional. Ensuring that their element of air can flow freely throughout their household may be an Aquarian's priority, so introducing the Chinese practice of feng shui into their home and office space could help restore some harmony.

Associated with blood circulation, an adrenaline fuelled sport that gets an Aquarian's blood pumping could be how this energetic sign likes to stay fit and healthy. This alternative air sign might literally be in their element taking on daring sports like base jumping or paragliding. Or if heights aren't an Aquarian's thing, skiing or snowboarding off-piste somewhere a little different in the world might be more suited to this unconventional sign. After an active day on the slopes, a little *après-ski* sauna will no doubt be where Aquarians make a beeline for in order to give their tired muscles and blood circulation that extra boost.

Having a healthy cholesterol level is essential for everyone wanting to live a long and healthy life, but it may be something that this sign is more keenly aware of to keep their associated body system of blood circulation thriving. Eating healthily is a great way to feel healthier and a proven way to naturally lower high cholesterol, so if this is a concern for any star sign, reducing their intake of foods that are high in saturated fats such as red meat and cheese is always a good place to start. Making a few adjustments to diet, such as ordering the tuna steak rather than the beef, should boost the body with healthier omega three fats and have any sign, Aquarius included, feeling much healthier. Aquarians should try not being a total stranger to their local GP, even if they prefer to practise alternative home remedies to battle the flu rather than get their annual jab, and always seek professional guidance if they have concerns about their health.

Mental health should be tended to just as readily as physical health and, as for any air sign, having a happy and clear mind is essential to an Aquarian's wellbeing. If an Aquarian's head is feeling clogged up with stress or worries, their usually innovative and free-flowing ideas can feel blocked, which can compound an air sign's anxiety. Identifying the root of the problem could be the first step as the cause of anxiety may or may not be obvious. By tackling issues candidly, an Aquarian can then plan the most practical route to a happy solution, which could include turning to their beloved community, be it a neighbour or sibling, and asking for help.

Aquarius

· · · · · · · · · · · · · · · · ·

DAILY FORECASTS
for 2022

OCTOBER

Saturday 1st

Communications may go awry today so don't hit send before
you check a message. This is a frustrating day for getting
things done and connecting with your path. Use the time
to have some light-hearted pleasure without committing
to anything too heavy or draining. Feelings may be
misunderstood if expressed to the wrong people.

Sunday 2nd

Mercury is direct now and you may have a startling epiphany
about your personal path. This may also involve seeing things
from a new perspective. You will have time to adjust to this
and go back over something that has evaded you. Alone time
will help clear your thoughts.

Monday 3rd

You begin the working week with a sense of satisfaction. There
is excitement within your family so expect a few surprises.
Your tribe may pull together to make something happen or to
pull apart an outdated way of being. A home makeover could
be the project you are all involved in.

Tuesday 4th

Changes are happening for you. You may have an emotional
investment here and be unsure of how you feel. Let this
happen organically as by evening you may see the benefits.
Your sense of justice may be rattled but will be balanced out if
you think things through before acting.

Wednesday 5th

You may need to halt progress and evaluate things so far. This is not a bad thing as it will enable you to see where you may have been too impatient and chosen badly. You may be asked to step up and own your responsibilities. Put your money where your mouth is.

Thursday 6th

Today the energy is relatively gentle, and you may find that you enter a dreamy frame of mind. You may also feel cut off from reality. Take off the rose-tinted glasses and dream by all means, but keep one foot on the ground. Make sure you don't overspend today.

Friday 7th

If you listen very carefully, you may get a message or two from your inner voice. This may appear as critical, in which case you are doing yourself a disservice. Find the voice that is celebrating the work you have done on your triggers and traumas and reward yourself for your efforts.

Saturday 8th

You are re-aligned with your inner compass now. This will always fluctuate as you have mundane duties to get on with as well as your own personal growth. Your head and heart are not in sync today, so concentrate on one or the other. This evening you may think more clearly.

. . . .

Sunday 9th

A full moon in your communications area will show how you have made plans and followed or abandoned them. You may now see that you are prone to taking on too much without considering the longevity of your plans. Pluto turns direct and will help to make change more permanent.

Monday 10th

You are driven to move forward with a romance or creative project now. You need to have your voice heard and can be too boisterous and assertive. Slow down, charging in without all the facts will only muddle things up. What is so urgent that you risk a knockback?

Tuesday 11th

Your inquiring mind is very active now. You may wish to look at a course of higher education in something that fascinates you. Broadening your mind or reading around a new topic may help to balance and focus your intent. You may have a calling to travel today.

Wednesday 12th

Get on the right side of someone in authority such as a boss or spiritual leader. You may be challenging this person or asking questions to deepen your knowledge. However, you may be so keen to learn that you are pushing triggers or crossing boundaries. Take it one step at a time.

Thursday 13th

Catching up with a loved one may bring fun and laughter today. Conversations may be quirky or deep. Both are good and will be satisfying. You may be more optimistic and your creativity will be boundless. Explore all your options and see if you can find ones you hadn't previously considered.

Friday 14th

Your ruler, Saturn, may be showing you another lesson today. This will be about emotions and desires. You can't always get what you want, no matter how much you fawn and coax someone. Find the middle ground and make a compromise.

Saturday 15th

Today you may be lost in illusion or simply on cloud nine with a partner. Your sexual energy is high, and you wish to connect with your partner in a way that is both sensual and mutually protective. Get all your provisions and lock both of you away from the outside world.

Sunday 16th

Comfort and security are what you crave. It is time to assess the value of a relationship and what you can both bring to it. Who looks after who? Are you both rowing the boat? Do you feel as if you are doing all the work? Talk about this with ease.

Monday 17th

You may feel triggered today and will need to do some work on this. How does your personal safety impact on your need for control? This may be your ego talking and if so, this is a superficial need and one you can do without. Self-protection may be exaggerated now.

Tuesday 18th

Important relationships are a big issue. You desire to be seen in the spotlight and this may conflict with your partner's needs. Your self-expression may not do you any favours today as you will be unfiltered and say exactly what you mean. This may not be kind or respectful.

Wednesday 19th

You may have to come face-to-face with your own limitations today. This will not be easy for you, but you must remember that there are people who can help. There is no need to talk about it as your closest friends will simply know and offer you the support you need.

Thursday 20th

Mars and Venus give you a helping hand. Harmony may be restored and your passion for love and creativity burn again. It's possible that you have stepped up another notch on your personal path and have become more humble. This evening you are willing to return favours.

Friday 21st

Enjoy a day with easy energy. This is a rare chance to sit back and let your mind and heart mull over the recent past and upcoming future. You may feel inclined to do something which will benefit your health as you may have neglected it recently. Introspection comes naturally today.

Saturday 22nd

Today you can look at your inner compass from an objective viewpoint. You know that it is always there and are learning that some days you have more energy to work on it than others. This is an assessment day; make checks and gather resources for the road ahead.

Sunday 23rd

Your ruler turns direct today. Saturn has been in your sign for a long time and you may feel exhausted now. Spend time on self-love and treat yourself to something you desire. You may have intense feelings, but you need to slow down and breathe deeply.

Monday 24th

Your head and heart are having a little talk today. Just make sure that what you are hearing is not your inner critic. Listen to your heart and ignore words of self-doubt or negativity. Find a balance between personal time and couple time and you will achieve more successful outcomes.

Tuesday 25th

A new moon and solar eclipse may bring up intense emotions in the workplace. You may see issues of jealousy or control. Females will be highlighted. You may use these themes to make goals and intentions for career advancement, but avoid any drama or power struggles over the next two weeks.

Wednesday 26th

Hold on tight as this could be a day of volatile eruptions all over your workplace and family situations. An old issue from the past might resurface and you may find it difficult to deal with it in a helpful way. This is not a reflection on you personally, so stay strong.

Thursday 27th

You are in the mood for talking and intellectual discussion today. This will go down well in your social groups and you may find an outlet for your unexpressed worries. Online groups may be a place where you can share what you have learned about your personal growth this year.

Friday 28th

You may be tempted to make an impulse buy which is expensive and frivolous. You may have to chain your hands together and not let your wallet out of your pockets. It's possible that a spiritual group you were once interested in comes back into your awareness and you reconnect there.

Saturday 29th

Your energy may be very low. It's possible that you are drained or feel heavy and need to rest. This is essential to your mental health as you are about to enter a few days of introspection and need that time alone. Wind down and switch off from the world.

Sunday 30th

Mars turns retrograde today. You may notice that progress slows down which can be frustrating for a go-getter like you. Don't push romance now as it will push back. Looking after number one today may show you some unique new routines of self-care which will work for you.

Monday 31st

Hard work on your psyche no longer frightens you. You find another trigger and deal with it superbly. Not a lot is bothering you today and you are on top of your game. If your mood and mind seem at odds later, flow with them and see where they lead.

NOVEMBER

. . . .

Tuesday 1st

Everything seems like an uphill struggle today. The trick is not to take it personally. You may find that your duties are divided between home and work and you have difficulty making time for both. This will almost certainly tire you out, so make time for yourself at the end of the day.

Wednesday 2nd

What skills and talent can you revive today to help you with tasks? This may be anything which can restore balance and harmony in the workplace to money-making schemes. Your love life may be dragging you down and you are impatient to move forward. Accept that you can't right now.

Thursday 3rd

Today is much easier as you go with the flow more. Better communication is your most valuable asset now. You may notice that you are prioritising happiness over productivity, and this will be fine if it helps you to maintain a good balance of work and play.

Friday 4th

You manage to re-attach to your inner compass and have an emotional pull towards doing the things that you love. You may have to wait a while or accept that there are still small changes to be made before you can take that leap of faith and progress on your path.

Saturday 5th

Look out for irritations between home and work. You may be focusing on one side too much and neglecting the other. This will show up today and may cause you to re-think some strategies. It's impossible to please everyone but you do your best. Think about how you have managed this before.

Sunday 6th

Ensure that your conversations are clear today. You may come across as assertive or bossy in your love relationship. If you must play by the rules, then so must other people. It will ultimately benefit all to do so. Your mind may wander back into old hurts later.

Monday 7th

Today you may find that your need to love everyone equally is not accepted by some. You may see issues of jealousy or possessiveness arise. Don't seduce or be enticed into something which may be underhand and sneaky. It won't make you feel good in the long run.

Tuesday 8th

A full moon and lunar eclipse may show up how you have worked with your family or with things that you value. This could startle you into realising that some things are not worthy of your attention. Listen carefully for messages coming from your unconscious and take them seriously.

Wednesday 9th

Watch what you say today. There's a chance that gossip or rows can erupt and reveal deep secrets. This may begin a new process of letting something go as it no longer serves your best interests. Be discerning now and be kind if this includes people around you.

Thursday 10th

There is a double-edged feel to today. You may be dreaming or searching the depths of your psyche. As a result, you may find golden nuggets of wisdom that will be useful now. At the same time, you feel restricted in your enquiries as not everyone is willing to discuss certain issues.

Friday 11th

Be mindful of your energy levels today. You may desire to be romantic or creative, but you simply don't have any enthusiasm. This will pass but, in the meantime, allow yourself this precious downtime to check in with your health. If something is too big, leave it for another time.

Saturday 12th

You may wish to feel nurtured and protected today. This is a good weekend for feeding your soul or getting all your mundane jobs done. You may have a chance to talk with someone special about deep and mysterious issues which are fascinating you at the moment. Be imaginative and intuitive.

Sunday 13th

Continue doing things you love today. Good food and company can assist in elevating your mood and bringing pleasant surprises. Emotionally, you will be on cloud nine enjoying sharing secrets and desires with someone you admire. Just make sure to keep one foot on the ground, ready for the coming week.

Monday 14th

Your intuition is high today and you may expect to understand a lot more than you realise. However, your sense of justice is also keen, and you may have to deal with something unpleasant. Partner time is essential this afternoon as you need to sound off to someone you trust.

Tuesday 15th

It's possible that a jealousy or control issue arises in the workplace, possibly involving women. If you feel inclined to take this on yourself, you may make a formidable champion. It will rock some boats, but this may be needed.

Wednesday 16th

You may enter a time where your social life picks up pace. Make sure that you allow time for a partner too if they are not included in your wider groups. Communication needs to have absolute clarity today as there's a chance that you are tricked or deluded at work.

. . . .

Thursday 17th

Reach out to your circle of friends as this may help you to discuss difficult topics in a safe place. This may also involve social media interest groups. You may find that something has grabbed your attention and you wish to explore more. Going deep may be scary but will bring you new understanding.

Friday 18th

You may be extra tired today so check what is more important and what you can do another time. Concentrate on making time for yourself as others may need you to help with something you just don't have the energy for. Avoid being dragged into other's business.

Saturday 19th

Your energy may be so low that a day in bed with a good book is all you can do. You may find it hard to concentrate and prefer to watch TV instead. Your mind is full of nonsense and you need to separate fact from fiction. If friends call, join them.

Sunday 20th

Your energy returns as does your sense of duty and responsibility. You may now see the need to get out and do simple chores that will get you through the day. Working through a checklist will be satisfying. Balancing everyone's requirements is a lot easier than you first thought.

Monday 21st

The workplace is highlighted, and you may see people coming and going. Is there anything you have forgotten to do? There may be a deadline and extra effort is needed. Your social groups are getting chatty and you could be in demand more in the coming weeks.

Tuesday 22nd

The Sun moves into your friends zone to enhance the new activity there. The Moon, however, is making you look at past problems you have faced within your family group and work arena. These may have surfaced again, and you try to recall how you settled them previously. Little surprises may unsettle you.

Wednesday 23rd

Don't let your emotions guide you today. They are more inclined to drift into fantasy thinking and will be biased. You must get a grip on reality and check all the facts. From there, you can make an informed decision if one is needed. Friends may give you impartial advice.

Thursday 24th

A new moon in your friends zone is another chance to start something new and exciting with your social groups. You may desire to spread your wings a little and visit overseas friends or explore other cultures now. Jupiter turns direct and gives you a big green go-ahead sign.

Friday 25th

Any recent excitement may have exhausted you and you should pull back a little today. You need time to process new thoughts and plans. Try not to make any commitments and politely excuse yourself from groups until you have had time to yourself. They will be waiting when you are ready.

Saturday 26th

Today has gentle energy which will enable you to take stock of all that has happened recently. If you can switch off your natural bias and judgement and sit as an observer, you may be able to align yourself with new thoughts and perspectives. Make a plan for steps to take.

Sunday 27th

Some things become clear to you today. You may have had to swim through muddy waters to get there but you have. What do you need to lovingly release from your life so that you have room for something new? How can you do this in a fair manner?

Monday 28th

You wake feeling optimistic but tired. All this soul-searching and recycling of old patterns can be exhausting. However, if you refrain from making any major decisions just yet, you may sail through the day gently. If you feel stuck, stay there and look all around at what is challenging you.

Tuesday 29th

It may be that you are the centre of attention today which you enjoy. However, don't let this go to your head and stay humble. Conversations this evening may be tiresome or misunderstood. If someone is not hearing you, leave it and try again another day. Don't push it.

Wednesday 30th

You may have to lay the law down today if someone is being deliberately awkward. You can do this with compassion, so it won't be too bad. This may allow you to see that however much you value someone's presence, you are not their scapegoat. They must own responsibility too.

DECEMBER

. . . .

Thursday 1st

This is a very challenging day where stubbornness comes at you from all angles. You may have to divide your time between social groups and lovers. If you feel stuck in the middle, take a time-out and latch on to your inner compass. It's still there for whenever you need it.

Friday 2nd

Your dreams may be more vivid now and display the turbulence you are currently experiencing. Emotions when awake may be larger than usual as you try to connect to something surreal, possibly spiritual. Friends may inspire or ground you today. Be prepared to communicate your feelings to those close to you.

Saturday 3rd

A better day comes with easy interactions with your love life and social friendships. You may enjoy time with both or combine them. Maybe you take your lover to a party. Saturn, your ruler, is pleased with you for thinking of a solution to what may have been problematic.

Sunday 4th

Neptune turns direct today and your true north calls you once more. Your heart has a message for you, and you must listen carefully. This may involve a tweak of your plans, but this will benefit you in many ways. Be open to suggestions and advice now.

Monday 5th

Look to an elder or teacher who may offer you a lesson to put you back on track with self-development and following your dreams. You may have a sudden realisation of what it was you were meant to be doing all along. Unexpected help may come from family members today.

Tuesday 6th

Make sure that any plans and arrangements you have with friends are watertight as they may go astray over the coming festive season. You may need to make last-minute plans or cancellations. Big gestures are possible as you entertain the idea of spending time with a lover or creative project later today.

Wednesday 7th

This is a simple day where you just have to get enough done to get by. There are no major issues to deal with, but you may find that your mind turns inward and you are processing a lot of information. Hidden things will surface to be healed now.

Thursday 8th

A full moon in your romance zone shows you how much you have worked on love and creativity this year. Self-expression is also a theme and you may say something you have been longing to voice now. This may fill you with anticipation, but you are relieved when it is out there.

Friday 9th

You may be left feeling vulnerable and exposed today. Find your comfort zone and operate from inside its safety. You are not under attack, but you will function better if you believe you are safe. However, your heart may still give the game away as you speak your truth.

Saturday 10th

Today begins a few weeks of total self-love and care. It's possible that a lot of material comes up from your psyche now because you are in the right frame of mind to deal with it and heal it. You have all the resources you need to transform old wounds into a new you.

Sunday 11th

Let go of something you are fighting to control. You may not be meant to be in charge here. It's likely that you are clinging on to something that is no longer a fit. Let it go with love and grieve if you need to.

Monday 12th

You may feel uncomfortable and not know which way to turn. Look to your partner for comfort and support. Validation too if you feel the need for it. You wish to be outgoing and optimistic, but this needs a little extra effort. Success will come when you stay responsible and dutiful.

Tuesday 13th

Family members may be causing a disturbance which may make you want to rebel. Don't do it as this will drain your energy and make your boundaries weak. Stand up for your rights and be an example to others. Don't take on unnecessary baggage as it will weigh you down.

Wednesday 14th

Practice self-care today and have time alone if you need it.
Something as simple as cooking a favourite meal and a pamper
before bedtime will soothe those midweek blues. Grounding
activities can also help you to come back to your centre of
calm and positivity. Give it a try.

Thursday 15th

There is a huge amount of earthy energy today which you
may not like. However, right now you may be flying too far
away and need to come back to base. You may be surprised
at how much this helps, and can talk to others about your
inner work.

Friday 16th

If you need to make yourself small and invisible today, you
can do this by managing your everyday duties and leaving
dreaming for another time. You may feel more productive if
you knuckle down to the daily grind and declutter ready for
the festive season. It will also make you feel fresh.

Saturday 17th

You may not be in the mood for either love or family matters
today. Creative and romantic pursuits may weigh heavy on you
as will introspection. The best thing you can do now is to let
your mind explore the possibility of bringing more harmony
into your life.

Sunday 18th

A day of duty and responsibility awaits you. There are some things you just can't change so don't waste your energy trying. Reach out to other lands or cultures to satisfy an itch you may have regarding higher education, religion or philosophies.

Monday 19th

Today you have an intense frame of mind which will help to get your work done. You may have a razor-sharp perception of the more difficult challenges in the workplace, but you get to the bottom of them easily. Let no one distract you from this as you will gain points from the boss and be seen in a favourable light.

Tuesday 20th

You have many big ideas today, but don't be in a rush to implement them, they can wait. Family obligations arise and cause tension. These can be appeased by letting others know that you have stuff to do and will return later to see to their needs.

Wednesday 21st

The winter solstice arrives with the shortest day and this may make you hurry through your chores. A midweek social event may be nice as will a time to rest. Pause, reflect and contemplate on the year gone by, and congratulate yourself on how much you have grown and developed your inner world.

Thursday 22nd

There is no time for dreaming as you may have deadlines to meet before the holidays. You are more than ready for a break, but you are also conscious of what needs to be done first. Put family and romantic matters on hold until you have done your work.

Friday 23rd

There is a new moon today which can help you set goals and intentions regarding your private, inner life. Self-development is an ongoing process and when you see how far you have come this year you will be willing to dig even deeper to become the best version of you yet.

Saturday 24th

It will be difficult to find time for you today but when you do, it will be worth it. Your heart and mind are in sync and allow you to feel good about yourself. A great sense of where you are and where you are heading lets you dream a little today.

Sunday 25th

Enjoy the festive fun. Your self-control will help you to contribute to the celebrations and do your bit without complaint. There is plenty of love to go around and you may be the one who is giving it. Keep a little back for yourself.

Monday 26th

Watch your energy levels today as your family may be demanding too much from you. This may result in a mini tantrum just to blow off steam. Stay out of aggravations that don't involve you and make sure that personal boundaries are strong and protected. Be mature and responsible at this time.

Tuesday 27th

This is a dreamy day when you can kick back and relax. You may wish to do this alone or with someone very special. It might be a time where you choose to do some introspection that has a more spiritual element. Place real value on the connections you make.

Wednesday 28th

Your inner compass and true north are waiting for you today. You may find that you have already made plans for next year which will help you to follow your dreams and visions. If the festive season is tiring you, withdraw and practise self-care today as it will balance you.

Thursday 29th

Just as the year is almost finished, Mercury turns retrograde. This may not be so bad as it will involve your private life. You may feel that this gives you a chance to re-visit what has surfaced for you and to assess its new meaning in your life.

Friday 30th

Although your energy is telling you to run, you may just have
to walk today as your goals are not visible and you will have
to wait. Slow down the pace and enjoy the remainder of the
holidays. Romance can be satisfying but not as exciting as you
would like.

Saturday 31st

Don't let anyone tell you how to enjoy the last day of 2022.
You may have a testing time or be in demand from different
quarters. If you desire to stay in and have an early night, then
do it. Take care of yourself and see to your own needs.

Aquarius

· · · · · · · · · · · · · · ·

DAILY FORECASTS
for 2023

JANUARY

. . . .

Sunday 1st
The stars are encouraging you to rest today. You may start to feel more restless as the day goes on, but take it easy and chill out. Make a New Year's resolution to stop making the same mistakes when it comes to romance, as a positive new love wave is on the way.

Monday 2nd
Start the day with meditation, or any ritual that works for you and encourages you to be quiet and still the mind. There may be a part of you that wants to be alone today, but getting together with family is recommended. This is even more important if you're feeling lonely.

Tuesday 3rd
It might be the right time to declare your affections or let someone know you love them. If you've been keeping quiet about romance, it's all change today as love planet Venus enters your star sign. If you want to quit an on-off relationship, take decisive action this evening.

Wednesday 4th
It's an excellent date for communication and connection. If you're looking for love, make your intentions known – join a dating site or ask someone out. If you're in a long-term relationship or marriage, make time for romance and use the right words to show your appreciation for your partner.

Thursday 5th

It's a lively time for home and family matters as it's in these
key areas of your life where change is on the cards. Perhaps
you're ready to embrace a new chapter, or a new home or
family situation. Keep moving forward and do what's right for
you and the ones you love.

Friday 6th

Today's full moon highlights charity and humanitarian goals,
which taps into the side of your nature that cares about society
and the world you live in. You may consider volunteering or
helping other people out in some way. The more you give, the
more you could receive in return.

Saturday 7th

There could be news about work or a health-related issue
during this full moon phase. Listen to your head and your
heart when making key decisions and do what's right for you.
It's time to let go of past concerns and put your wellbeing first.

Sunday 8th

You may feel something of an outsider at the moment if your
beliefs or interests contrast with those of the people around
you. Recent events could confirm where you're on track and
where you're off-piste. Talk to the people concerned without
playing the blame game.

Monday 9th

Venus and Mars, the lovers of the heavens, are working
together today, so you may be tempted back into an on-off
relationship. Ideally, wait until the weekend before making
a move. If you're a parent, be there for a child who may be
struggling – action speaks louder than words.

Tuesday 10th

You may experience some sadness around a close relationship today. Endings are never easy and letting go takes time. Deal with practical matters to take your mind off what's bothering you. If you don't want to feel the depth of your emotions, use diversion tactics for now.

Wednesday 11th

It may sometimes seem as though you're having the same conversation over and over, but that's not the point. What matters is experiencing that close connection and the safety and security that family or old friends bring. Return to the person in your life who knows you the best.

Thursday 12th

Something that's been stuck since November 2022 is starting to break open. If you've been dealing with writer's block recently, you could experience a shift in your creative energy today. It's an ideal date for being assertive in your communications, especially with a loved one.

Friday 13th

You're more of a dreamer today and you may feel wistful about your life or the year ahead. Play around with ideas, visualise what you want to bring forth and allow yourself to dream. Love is moving in the right direction and a meeting of minds could reveal that you're back on track.

Saturday 14th

Take yourself off somewhere different today. If you're with someone you cherish, so much the better. There's a sweetness to your stars and a happy-go-lucky vibe to your weekend. Be around those people who lift your spirits, or treat yourself and the ones you love to a meal out.

Sunday 15th

There's an unpredictable side to your nature that craves freedom. That's all well and good, but some relationships thrive best on trust and loyalty, commitment and monogamy. Be honest with yourself and what you want when it comes to love, and try not to fall into bad habits.

Monday 16th

It's a good day to focus on your work and career, your future and where you're heading. You may have to be something of a magician at work if you're wearing many different hats. Try to leave your personal life out of your professional life and concentrate on doing your job well.

Tuesday 17th

You may be completing a job or project today, or it could be a key period of preparation for a new chapter in your life. You'll get more done today if you switch off your phone and find somewhere quiet to work. Avoid distraction.

Wednesday 18th

Mercury's change of direction could bring the news or information you've been waiting for. This might help you resolve a personal issue or enable you to make a tough decision. Alternatively, you could recognise that you're living too much in the past rather than focusing on the future.

Thursday 19th

Hang out with your friends and put the world to rights. If you're typical of your star sign, you're often interested in politics, social, environmental and humanitarian issues. If you feel you've not been doing enough to help recently, that's all about to change and soon.

Friday 20th

If you haven't yet set any New Year's resolutions, now is the time to do so as the Sun's move into Aquarius is the start of your birthday month. You may sense that you're coming back out into the world. Create some time this weekend to set intentions for your year ahead.

Saturday 21st

The more you can be true to yourself and express your identity and personality, the more your personal goals can mesh and come together. Today's new moon could coincide with a remarkable opportunity where you get a chance to make your mark.

Sunday 22nd

Unexpected events could throw your weekend plans into upheaval. You might hear about someone close to you who's moving, or maybe you could be the one who's ready to swing into action and start a family or find somewhere new to live.

Monday 23rd

Listen carefully to your instincts during this period of change. You could be the one holding everything together, and other people may turn to you as the voice of reason. This would be a good time to sign up for a course or workshop and focus on your personal development.

Tuesday 24th

You may know that a relationship situation has to change. For some of you, this is a time when you're right to decide whether you commit or quit. A friends-with-benefits arrangement may be tempting, but it's important to consider the feelings of all people concerned, yourself included.

Wednesday 25th

A new opportunity could take you away from your daily routine and is worth following up on. It's a great time for activities that make you feel good. Crank up your self-care and engage in any area of your life that pleases you. A partner's generosity restores your faith in love.

Thursday 26th

Remind yourself of simple pleasures, put enjoyment high on your list of priorities and savour life fully. You may not know where you're going to end up, but does that matter if you're living well in the present? At least aim to enjoy the ride and open up your world.

Friday 27th

Venus' move into your money zone is good news and could bring financial help or support your way. This is a time to trust in life and have faith that things will work out for the best. Look after your affairs and dismiss any advice that's not helpful.

Saturday 28th

It may be that you don't see eye-to-eye with a relative at the moment, or perhaps there's someone in your life who has a different attitude to your own. This will become evident if it's a clash of security over freedom, or conventionality over an alternative path.

Sunday 29th

Society often expects you to fit in and do what everyone else does. If you're a typical Aquarius, you'll have your own set of beliefs and opinions about what's right and wrong. You may find it a challenge not to confront someone who thinks they're better than you are.

Monday 30th

Something is shifting and ready to break free. You may be thinking about a personal situation that crops up continually and won't go away, or maybe you're looking back at your past and the beliefs that were ingrained in you as a child. There's a theme of karma in your life.

Tuesday 31st

You have a passionate nature, and your drive and ambition require a constructive outlet. It could be a creative hobby, familial love, a steamy affair that refuses to die or a craving for excitement and good times. Do what's right for you.

FEBRUARY

Wednesday 1st

If you're worried about money or a personal issue, take practical steps to get yourself back on track. It can help to write things down, get organised and work out a plan. Keep your attention firmly focused on your long-term goals and work steadily towards them.

Thursday 2nd

It's important to think about the news or information coming into your life. Some advice you're receiving isn't relevant now and could work against you. Don't just believe that everything's going to be okay; use your common sense and keep it real.

Friday 3rd

Sometimes, you need to expand your knowledge and be open-minded to new ways and means of living vibrantly. Step out of your comfort zone and try something new. If you're dealing with a fitness issue, this is a good date to consider trying a new workout if your current routine isn't working.

Saturday 4th

Today's astrology triggers your inner rebel. You might be breaking away from past ties, or wanting freedom from something that's holding you back. This could be linked to a home or family situation, or it might be about your attitude and wanting to try to do things differently.

Sunday 5th

Use the full moon in the sky to bring clarity and insight to your relationship situation. If something's off, examine it fully. Someone else in your life could take centre stage now and there may be a reason to celebrate, but ensure you have your chance to shine as well.

Monday 6th

There could be a resolution today regarding events that took place on or around Christmas Day last year. You may have a greater understanding of what was happening back then, or perhaps your spiritual path has deepened as a result. Acknowledge what you've learned.

Tuesday 7th

Emotions remain lively today and any disagreements could come to a head. Someone may pick an argument with you, or you might have had enough of a tricky situation and decide to challenge a loved one or housemate. Be firm but fair, and step carefully around anger issues.

Wednesday 8th

Take a close look at your finances today. Other people may have their ideas of what's right for you but you're wise to trust your instincts. Someone at home or in your family could be the catalyst for good fortune.

Thursday 9th

You might have to ask an awkward question today and you mustn't shy away from a taboo area. You could be studying hard or researching for a job or project. It's a good day for a task that requires concentration, even if you do feel bored or unmotivated at times.

Friday 10th

It seems as if there's a lot to think about and a personal issue could weigh heavy. You might be worried about someone who you fear might not be entirely on your side. Keep your suspicions to yourself for now and wait to see what's revealed.

Saturday 11th

Your confidence gets a welcome boost today as talk planet Mercury enters your star sign. This is the time to find your voice, speak up, and focus on your personal goals. Leave the past behind and look to the future. Put yourself and your own needs first.

Sunday 12th

It's a good day to think about your career and your future path. If your goals have shifted recently, try not to stay locked on autopilot but take some time out to review what's up next. Be wary of a family member who may persist in trying to steer you down a different track.

Monday 13th

It's hard to remain motivated and inspired if what you do for a living doesn't fit with who you are as a person. This could bother you more than you may realise, and things might come to a head over the next few days. Be clear about your purpose in a role of responsibility.

Tuesday 14th

When you find your community in life, your happiness levels take an upward swing. Being around the right people today sets you on the right path, so find the people whose ideas and beliefs fit your own. Your Valentine's Day crush may remain elusive – think hidden dreams.

Wednesday 15th

At its best, today's stars indicate that you may find yourself in a place where you trust that life will provide for you and things will work out for you. Your finances could prove to be inspirational and/or uncertain today.

Thursday 16th

Life could take a serious turn today. If you're considering the bigger picture, it could help to draw up long-term plans for your future rather than allowing fear or doubt to take over. Get your business head on and apply it to your personal life.

Friday 17th

Take some time out for yourself to process recent events. There might not be any easy answers, but quiet time could help you come to terms with what's happening in your life. Do whatever's necessary and regain your strength, either physical or emotional.

Saturday 18th

Knowledge is power. You could hear something liberating today that leads you to a breakthrough. Open your eyes and ears, read and research, and listen out for wisdom and expertise. A conversation within your community could have a brilliant outcome.

Sunday 19th

If you want to revolutionise your earning potential or your ability to make money, you must be up to date with the latest technologies and ideas. Keep one step ahead and find out about future trends. Pay close attention to the flow of cash in and out of your life.

Monday 20th

Today's new moon puts the spotlight on your values and what's important to you. You might be changing what you think you want or need. Be savvy in your financial dealings and balance a caring heart with a logical brain.

Tuesday 21st

It's important to be flexible if you're involved in negotiations regarding your home or family. Things could change quickly and you might hear unexpected news that requires a radical rethink. Try not to overreact if someone close to you goes back on their word.

Wednesday 22nd

There are some lovely opportunities today as long as you're out and about in your neighbourhood. You might meet someone delightful close to home, or have a heart-warming encounter with a neighbour, relative or sibling. You may know what to say to motivate a loved one.

Thursday 23rd

The positive vibes continue today, so make the most of it.
If you're finding your voice online, it's a good day to reach
more people and connect with them, potentially via a blog or
social media. Sometimes, it doesn't take a lot to put a smile on
someone's face.

Friday 24th

You may be pulled back towards the past, whether
you're sorting out mementoes and family possessions or
remembering someone you've lost. Your current role might
be to ensure things are put in their rightful place. Take care of
loved ones and honour your family's legacy.

Saturday 25th

You're like a whirlwind today, bringing something new and
different into the family or your home. You're a future-
oriented individual; even though the past has created who you
are now, it's your aspirations and who you're becoming that
are most significant.

Sunday 26th

There are some days when you have to put your beliefs to one
side to accommodate others. That might mean prioritising
another person's wants and needs above your own. Keep your
opinions to yourself for harmony's sake.

Monday 27th

You may not want to be reminded about the serious side of life today; instead, you're determined to have a good time whatever happens. Think about ways you can do more of what makes you happy, even if that means doing it on the cheap. Smile and the world smiles back at you.

Tuesday 28th

You may feel a surge of energy or excitement today. This might be linked to your relationship with a child and what's happening in their life. You may have a burning desire to talk to someone close – perhaps a lover. Be proactive and wake up determined to have a good day.

MARCH

Wednesday 1st

Ideally, you want an easy day where you can get on with things and not too much is expected of you. If you didn't sleep well, focus on what needs to be done and nothing more. It's a good day to boost your emotional wellbeing, so do something that's good for you.

Thursday 2nd

This could be a glorious day for love and relationships. You might meet someone new and experience an instant connection. There could be good news for a relative or neighbour. If you don't respond as other people expect, it might be because you're in a reflective mood.

Friday 3rd

Focus on the basics of life; eat well, sleep well, and take some daily exercise. It's a time when you could easily slip into bad habits but that's not wise; instead, make a concerted effort to take good care of yourself. A problem shared could be a problem halved, so talk your worries through with a loved one.

Saturday 4th

Prioritise love and your relationships. Spend time with someone with an infectious sense of fun who knows how to make you feel better immediately. That may not necessarily be the person you live with or a member of your family.

Sunday 5th

This is a transitional phase in the year, and you may already sense that you need to look closely at certain areas in your life. Be in your heart more than your head so you focus on your emotional needs. Try to switch off from the world today and be with the person you love the most.

Monday 6th

Draw up a plan of action if you have any money worries. Burying your head in the sand or leaving important letters unopened isn't a helpful strategy. Instead, use this week's full moon to review your situation and plan out what can be done about it.

Tuesday 7th

If you've been dealing with hardship in your life recently like an ailing parent or a low mood, you may be glad to see the back of Saturn from your star sign. However, if you've grown in authority and been successful, you may feel that you want to keep that momentum going.

Wednesday 8th

Work out what your future plans are and make a list of goals to help you achieve them. Saturn's major move into your money zone either means you could be establishing yourself financially or that you have to rein in your spending.

Thursday 9th

You may become aware of where your knowledge is lacking today, which might lead you to research study courses or to brush up on your qualifications. This may be important to you for travel reasons or because you want to be on the move in your career.

Friday 10th

You may feel pleased for another person if you hear that they've done well in life or they're starting a family. However, there could be a small part of you that's envious or compares you to them detrimentally. Try not to fall into this trap and focus instead on your positive emotions.

Saturday 11th

It's potentially a day of agreement and accord. You might learn a lot about another person that adds to your understanding of the world. You could meet someone new and click with them immediately. A clever money-making idea may be on the cards.

Sunday 12th

Your overactive mind could stop you from getting a good night's sleep, especially if you have a lot to consider. You may have a new career or vocational path in mind and want to get another opinion. Help is at hand, however, so turn to other people for ideas and support.

Monday 13th

If you're hanging out with the rich crowd, it's important to double-check whether you can live up to other peoples' lifestyles. Make time to review your social life and how much you benefit from those outings. Having the right group of friends could make a big difference.

Tuesday 14th

Today's stars create a potentially dreamy atmosphere, although it's not the time to get carried away when it comes to love. Enjoy yourself but keep your expectations realistic. A third party may be a seductive influence, but you're wise to veer away from a situation that smacks of scandal.

Wednesday 15th

Someone close could be your saviour or help to bring clarity to your current situation. It's a good date to reach out and ask for help if you need it. There's no shame in admitting where you may have gone wrong.

Thursday 16th

You could be pulled in all kinds of different directions today. A lot is going on, and various people will require your time, attention or support. Try to be detached when advising on other people's problems and don't get overly involved.

Friday 17th

Look for the safety and stability in your life in relation to your home and family. If a child is causing an issue or acting out, get your partner or a third party in to help you resolve the problem and restore harmony. You can't do this all on your own.

Saturday 18th

As an Aquarius, you are one of the social signs of the zodiac, so spending time alone can sometimes be testing for you. Dig deep this weekend and think of this period as a time of rebirth and renewal. Do whatever you choose in order to learn to love and protect yourself.

Sunday 19th

Talk planet Mercury moves into your communication zone today. You may discover your ideal role close to home or within your community over the next weeks. It's a time when you could get a clearer understanding of your purpose or calling moving forward.

Monday 20th

Today is the equinox and officially the start of the spring. This is when the Sun moves into Aries, the first sign of the zodiac, so there's a sense of a fresh start. Your communication and community zones are lit up with a lively vibe, so make the most of it.

Tuesday 21st

Today's new moon is excellent for sowing seeds, speaking up and finding your voice. It's all about the new, whether you're making new connections, or coming up with an innovative idea or something unique to say. Find the people who can help you and ask for what you need.

Wednesday 22nd

It's an excellent date to initiate a conversation, start a debate and generally get the ball rolling. You might have tons of ideas that require focus or direction. If so, jump to it. The more expansive your reach, the more likely your chance of good fortune. Don't be shy.

Thursday 23rd

You have two options. One is to step into your power, even if what you're required to say is unpopular or taboo. The other is to allow society to dictate to you and crush you under its weight. It's a big ask, but you may be starting to realise that recent events have been leading you to this moment.

Friday 24th

It may feel as if you have one foot in the past and one foot in the future. The best way forward is to honour both. Take a move in the right direction but don't dismiss what's been and gone. The past has made you who you are but new horizons beckon.

Saturday 25th

What's new in your life? What are you beginning? This could be starting your own family, buying a house or leaving home for the first time. Alternatively, you may be starting a new job, debuting a new haircut, or getting fit for a charity challenge. On your marks, get set, go!

Sunday 26th

You may fancy some downtime today, especially if life has been full of epic events of late. Give yourself time to acknowledge what you've achieved and be kind to yourself regarding any recent mistakes. It's an ideal day to take it easy and watch TV or chill with your loved ones.

Monday 27th

This is an excellent time to make new friends and join in with your local community. It will not only be enjoyable but potentially inspiring, as new ideas could come your way thick and fast. You may have more than one innovative project you're interested in starting or contributing to.

Tuesday 28th

If you're a student or teacher, this is a top date for education, and a good time for a test or exam. You not only have plenty of get-up-and-go, but your ideas are focused and structured, which is a great combination. Jump to it and get things done.

Wednesday 29th

If you're starting a family business, or you and your loved ones are helping each other out in another way, you're in tune with your stars. Equally, the more you aim to create a family atmosphere at work, the happier you all are and the more you get done.

Thursday 30th

It may sound obvious, but the more fun you're having, the more productive you are. A steady job can provide the financial stability you crave but it's not the only way of winning resources. For that, look to your family or your home.

Friday 31st

End the month on a high and line up a special event with your other half or in your local community. People matter today and you'll be in a better mood when you're out and about having fun. Be open to laughter, initiate new opportunities, and make the most of life.

APRIL

Saturday 1st
You may prefer to meet new people today rather than getting together with family or close friends. It's a good date for learning and gaining knowledge. Take a trip to your library or check out your local bookshop. Commit to studying something new with your other half.

Sunday 2nd
If you're dealing with any life admin, it could take longer than you expect. It's wise to get on top of filing or correspondence, but do ensure you have some time for yourself as well. You might be contemplating the best way to pass on some difficult news.

Monday 3rd
You may be considering how to ditch a habit or introduce a ritual into your life that enables you to let go of the past and move on. This could involve releasing an out-of-date mindset or letting go of negativity. You may find it easier to stick to whatever you commit to today.

Tuesday 4th
If you're good with paperwork, get on top of your future planning. Alternatively, you may be helping someone else out with their plans, perhaps a parent or another member of your family. Don't let cash slip through your fingers because your accounts aren't up to date.

Wednesday 5th

Talk planet Mercury is going to be in your home and family zone for an unusually long time. This indicates that you might have some ongoing negotiations or discussions regarding these key areas of your life. Make any important moves in these areas before April 21st.

Thursday 6th

Today's full moon highlights education, which is ideal for committing to a course of study or passing on what you know. You may have to read or find out more to make sense of what's happening. Be part of the world and decide where you can do your bit to help.

Friday 7th

If you're travelling and going to see family this Easter weekend, you're in tune with your stars. Even though it's the holiday weekend, stay focused on what's next in your life and plan accordingly. This is a lovely date for beautifying your home or consulting an interior designer.

Saturday 8th

The day could start well if you're painting and decorating, or helping another member of your family with their job, work or project. You could get things moving quickly and efficiently now, but be wary that not everything will go according to plan. You're wise to be flexible later on.

Sunday 9th

Your ideas may clash with other people's, especially someone in your family. It might be wise to meet up with a friend instead and change your surroundings. Take care you don't slip into a low mood later on.

Monday 10th

You have a clear day to do whatever you want. Ideally, catch up with good friends – perhaps someone who lives abroad or a study buddy. It's a good day to broaden your horizons and find out more about the lives of other people in different cultures.

Tuesday 11th

It's an ideal date to learn a language, widen your social network or extend your business connections. Wherever your life would benefit by reaching out to more people, this is a good time to go for it. Love, too, is looking positive, especially when you meet someone new.

Wednesday 12th

You could end up working overtime or feeling stressed if you've got too much on your plate today. Try to focus on one task at a time rather than attempting to get everything done at once. Support is at hand from someone closer to home than you might imagine. Even a quick chat could help.

Thursday 13th

You may not feel like being overly social and would rather spend time on your own. This might be because you're tired or under the weather, or perhaps you have some pent-up emotions that you find challenging when you're around other people. Retreat if you can.

Friday 14th

It's important to be firm with a loved one if their spending gets out of hand. It might be up to you to step in and take charge to stop them being frivolous, however challenging that may be.

Saturday 15th

The day gets better as it goes on. Keep busy and make an effort to connect with other people, whether on the phone or close to home. The more you reach out and share kindness, the more you benefit in return. A teaching or mentoring role could bring you fulfilment.

Sunday 16th

This isn't the time to let things slip; you're wise to draw up a long-term plan for the future and ensure you're on track to reach your goals. A sensible approach to finances works best now. A late-night phone call cheers you up no end.

Monday 17th

If you want to earn more money, it's an excellent day to get into that mindset and chase a higher salary. Release any past beliefs that hold you back and renew your vision and sense of purpose.

Tuesday 18th

You'll be happier having a chat than investing too much energy into work or chores. There could be some juicy gossip doing the rounds, or you might hear something that makes you realise you need to contact someone in your life – and fast. Jump to it!

Wednesday 19th

This isn't the time to go it alone. Instead, strengthen your close relationships and get to know the people within your community. Team up with others and work together towards a mutual cause. There's a theme of generosity, kindness and looking after one another today.

Thursday 20th

Communication is potentially life-changing during this eclipse week. You might experience a deep conversation with someone, or perhaps you witness a soulmate connection. What you discover could lead to good fortune. Your words have power.

Friday 21st

You may not see eye-to-eye with a member of your family or someone you live with today, or perhaps there are other reasons why your domestic life might not be peaceful or harmonious right now. Review your living situation over the next few weeks.

Saturday 22nd

Ideally, you require strong foundations, stability and calm in your life now. Retreat, go inward, buy more cushions – do whatever's necessary to slow you down and keep you comfortable. Say no to a social event if you know it would cost too much and tire you out.

Sunday 23rd

It's a better day for close relationships and social engagements. You may have got your energy back or rediscovered your va-va-voom. Love is in the ascendancy, so make the most of it – have fun with the one you love or ask someone out on a date.

Monday 24th

You may have to go back and renegotiate something this week, but don't rush into anything. Read the fine print and double-check what you're talking about. Things may not be exactly as they appear on paper.

Tuesday 25th

What you want and what you need are in flow. This is an excellent date to win others over to your way of thinking or bring people together in a happy union. You might experience this unity at home or within your place of work. Appeal to other people's emotions.

Wednesday 26th

Sometimes, good ideas come to you in the middle of the night, so you might be more than ready to leap into action today and get things moving. Whether you're keen to boost your health or get the job done, put your fired-up energy to good use.

Thursday 27th

You might recognise that your needs aren't being met in a relationship or business partnership, and you feel powerless to turn things around. You might want to end things, but be patient – you'll have a better chance of success in the second half of May.

Friday 28th

You could get caught up in the middle of a tricky family situation today, perhaps with your in-laws or an estranged relative. The situation may require careful navigation and negotiation, so take your time and consider who might be in the middle of it all.

Saturday 29th

Your best work ideas may come to you at the strangest times – in the shower, or while you're cooking, for example. Keep a notepad close by so you can jot your ideas down immediately. If you're in a relationship, chill with your other half without planning anything special.

Sunday 30th

You may have to look elsewhere today if you're stuck with life admin or lacking self-confidence. Find the person who can help you think things through systematically and is known to come up with the answers. Good old-fashioned common sense will set you straight.

MAY

....

Monday 1st

If tensions are building, turn your attention to the basics of life. Consider your foundations and what security means to you. You may be on the verge of changing direction in your work, home or family life. This could turn out to be a big week!

Tuesday 2nd

Aim to gain a new perspective on what's happening in your personal life. When you're at a crossroads, it's not always easy to know which direction is right for you. You may be under pressure now from other people, or perhaps you're the one who's putting pressure on yourself.

Wednesday 3rd

Things may be coming to a head at work and you might be ready to take a radical course of action. If tensions rise or office politics crank up a gear, this could be the final incident that pushes you over the edge. Find a constructive outlet for your anger – running could help.

Thursday 4th

Be wary around promises that can't be kept. Keep your wits about you, stay clever and bright, and keep close tabs on your finances. At the same time, you may experience a yearning to want to help other people.

Friday 5th

Today's lunar eclipse is about your home, your family and your past, as well as your career, your vocation and your future. These are the areas that may have gone through significant change since late 2021. What's already taken place could determine your next steps.

Saturday 6th

If your home and family affairs are dominating your life, it could be difficult to pursue your own vocation. If you know these areas are out of balance for you, play around with new ideas and see what's possible. Changes at home could act as a catalyst for personal transformation.

Sunday 7th

If you're meeting up and socialising with your work colleagues, you're in tune with your stars. Alternatively, you could meet someone today who works in the healthcare field and who might have some interesting facts and ideas to share with you.

Monday 8th

Keep an open mind today and be around other people who stimulate your thoughts and ideas. If you're typical of your star sign, you like to think outside of the box and you have an appreciation for all things unique and different. Push the boundaries of friendship.

Tuesday 9th

Being your true self might not be straightforward if other people in your life think you should do differently. What takes place now could be life-changing in that it helps you see yourself or others from a different angle.

Wednesday 10th

You're wise to keep things to yourself if someone at work keeps bothering you or irritating you. It won't be long now before you're able to find a way to distance yourself from this person or job. Try not to damage your career prospects by lashing out.

Thursday 11th

You may have so much going on at the moment that your mind is active in the middle of the night. Come the weekend, one issue may resolve itself without you having to lift a finger. Focus on yourself for now and your own needs. Do whatever's necessary to stay strong.

Friday 12th

It's not easy when you feel at odds with other people, or you find that you don't have much in common with your family or friends. It might be clear that some of your ideas are a bit out there, but stand up for yourself and stay true to your beliefs.

Saturday 13th

You may learn something about your relationship with money today. Perhaps you notice a frivolous side of your nature, for example, or someone could accuse you of not paying your way, which makes you realise how sensible you can be around money.

Sunday 14th

Think about what security means to you this weekend. Is it important for you to have a sanctuary and family or close friends nearby? Or are you happiest when you're independent and on the move? Focus your attention on these key areas.

Monday 15th

Talk planet Mercury turns direct in your home and family zone, so it's in these areas where you might feel as if a switch is flicked back on. News may come to light that helps you make a decision, possibly involving a family member or a property move.

Tuesday 16th

There's a link to your past and the place you come from. You might break free from past ties, take a step out on your own, or see your children fly the nest. If you've been thinking about making a trip back home, this is the year to make it happen.

Wednesday 17th

Actively engage with your next steps. You may be moving home, wanting to extend your property, or considering living abroad. You could welcome a new family member or even gain a lodger in your home. These areas are where opportunity lies.

Thursday 18th

If you're in any kind of power game, try not to charge in all guns blazing. The person you're up against may hold secrets and be willing to manipulate or control to get what they want. This is pertinent concerning your family relationships, an ex or other people close to you.

Friday 19th

Today's new moon is a symbol of new beginnings, and highlights your home and your family. Ask yourself relevant questions – what's changing in your life? What are you moving away from and what are you moving towards? Are you ready to leave the past behind?

Saturday 20th

This is potentially a romantic time for you. Mars, the planet linked to the libido, enters red-hot Leo and your relationship zone today, so it's an ideal time to focus on love. Allow yourself to be inspired by other people and pick up on their feel-good vibes.

Sunday 21st

Today, you could feel as though you want to take charge in a close relationship. However, be wary of power games and leave them out of your partnership; control issues should have nothing to do with love.

Monday 22nd

Today's stars are a healthier backdrop for a loving relationship full of truth and honesty. Be direct in your close relationships without losing the lightness and frivolity of love.

Tuesday 23rd

There's plenty of potential for adventure and passion today. You might be ready to introduce a new partner to your family, or a family member may have an announcement and some exciting news to share. There might be stirrings of an office romance as well.

Wednesday 24th

You may be in a competitive situation today, possibly within a work context or because you're entering a contest. Try not to get overly carried away by the thrill of winning, even if you would like to bring your opponent back down to earth.

Thursday 25th

Your emotions could be dependent on other people today, perhaps too much. This is all well and good if you're feeling passionate; not so nice if you're experiencing jealousy, resentment or rage. Notice your emotional response and how quickly your feelings can be triggered.

Friday 26th

It's worth acting quickly to try to sort out a misunderstanding at work. What may seem like a light flirtation to one person may be experienced differently by someone else. You may even be starting a relationship with a work colleague, but do keep your wits about you.

Saturday 27th

You're wise now to pay close attention to life admin and deal with any outstanding correspondence. If you haven't received a reply to a recent interaction, follow it up rather than assuming that everything's okay.

Sunday 28th

Saturn is sometimes thought of as the party pooper of the planets. When it's linked to your finances, it's wise to rein in your spending and keep close tabs on what's coming in and going out of your bank account – don't splash out on something you don't really need!

Monday 29th

Put your money where your mouth is today and be true to your word. You might be helping out a friend or a third party, or perhaps you need to hold yourself accountable on promises you've made to yourself. Be efficient and get things done.

Tuesday 30th

It's an excellent date to broach a relationship issue and resolve matters – and fast. If you're in a long-term relationship or marriage, consider your future plans as a couple. Think about how you can widen your experience of life through travel, study or learning a new skill together.

Wednesday 31st

You may realise that you want more from life today. This could come about because you're listening to a colleague at work or someone you meet in the gym. If their plans and ideas are exciting and adventurous, this could inspire you to reconsider your next steps.

JUNE

Thursday 1st

You may require complete quiet today in order to focus on the job at hand. You might not find that this concentration is easily come by, but do your best to find a quieter space. When you find your vocation in life, or a job that gives you meaning and purpose, then you can fly.

Friday 2nd

Disruptions at home or family dramas could get in the way of your work today. A conversation with a family member could confirm you're on different paths. If there's an inkling of romance at work, breathe it into life this evening.

Saturday 3rd

Know that this could be an emotional weekend with more than its fair share of drama. Make time for friendship – you might be hearing all about a good friend's love life today, or perhaps you're the one who has plenty to gossip about. Parties and celebration are on the cards, too.

Sunday 4th

Today's full moon is a time to consider your alliances and rethink your social circle. At the same time, recognise where your skills and talents are required and where you can make a name for yourself. What can you offer others? How can you more fully express yourself?

Monday 5th

Love planet Venus enters your relationship zone today, so the next few months could be extraordinary for one-to-one time with your close relationships. This is a reminder that you're at your best around other people rather than becoming overly analytical or introspective.

Tuesday 6th

Things could happen at lightning speed today and catch you unawares. There's potential for spontaneous conversations and impulsive decisions. You might be the one to leap in and offer advice, or perhaps someone in your family is the catalyst for dramatic change.

Wednesday 7th

You're back in the driving seat and potentially feeling more confident than you have for a while. If you've fallen head-over-heels for someone, this could leave you off balance. Intense emotions often take you by surprise, so do what you can to remain cool and calm.

Thursday 8th

You're one of the air signs, which means you're in your element when you talk, think and work things out. You're often more comfortable in your head, so you may be experiencing some instability or uncomfortable feelings because it's your heart that's in the process of being opened.

Friday 9th

Find time to talk to someone you live with, be they family or a housemate, as what you hear could prove insightful concerning values and your self-worth. Encourage the other person to pursue their dreams and be open to receiving their wisdom in return.

Saturday 10th

If it's proving a challenge to get through to a loved one, turn to someone else in the family to help. They may have an alternative way of communicating or connecting that works beautifully. You could find that you're too deeply enmeshed in whatever's going on.

Sunday 11th

Think of this period as a process of letting go. It's helpful to ditch what's no longer needed, whether it's intense emotions, resentment or actual real baggage. Declutter, detox, destress. Have one final conversation with someone in your life, then move on.

Monday 12th

Bring back the sunshine and let in the light. If personal issues have been heavy or stressful recently, or you've felt weighed down, state a positive intention to enjoy life more and keep things upbeat. Start by initiating a conversation that could lead to some fun and games.

Tuesday 13th

Put those fun plans in motion by sending out some invitations or setting up a group chat. It's an excellent date to market and sell, or to find the exact right person to meet your needs. Refuse to put up with time wasters and deal only with people who know their stuff.

Wednesday 14th

If you're in a relationship, your other half could be keen to start something new together, maybe linked to your home or families. You might feel things are moving too fast, however, so don't go along with anything that doesn't sit well with you. Be loving and kind, but firm.

Thursday 15th

You may have to lay down the law and put firm boundaries in place around money and spending, possibly with your child or partner, or maybe you could be the one who needs to rethink your outgoings and expenses. When in doubt, take the sensible route.

Friday 16th

Today offers an excellent opportunity to consider ways you can enjoy yourself that don't cost a fortune. If you've been overspending recently or finances are tight, research activities or a fun day out that won't blow your budget. You might have to suggest the same to a child.

Saturday 17th

There's a strong theme of partnership this weekend and learning to lean on someone close. This doesn't mean expecting them to do everything for you or sort out all your problems. Instead, it's about negotiation, communication and working things out together.

Sunday 18th

Today's new moon spells good news for love, whether romantic or platonic. It's a good time to be sociable. You might be naturally busy, juggling different areas of your life, or perhaps you want to actively improve your social life and arrange to see more of your friends.

Monday 19th

Don't allow yourself to be seduced into making promises you won't be able to keep, and play it safe when it comes to your purse strings. This is potentially a creative and inspirational time for you, so dream up a new venture or activity that could give you a boost.

Tuesday 20th

A family business could be on the cards, or perhaps you're looking at new ways to pool money and share resources with your family, your tenants or housemates. It's a good year to invest some time and love in your property.

Wednesday 21st

Look after yourself over the next few weeks and put your needs first. If you've been spending too much time and energy caring for others, readjust the balance. Equally, if you feel you need to be kinder and more caring to other people, do so.

Thursday 22nd

It's important to note that you're not the one in charge today; the emphasis sits firmly on other people and the roles they play in your life. Another person could initiate a thrilling night of love and passion.

Friday 23rd

Slow down over the weekend and turn your attention towards the things in life that ground you. This might be your vocation, your home or garden, your family or close friends. If you're seeking comfort in life, do more of what nurtures you.

Saturday 24th

Turn your attention to your finances, especially if you're running short of cash or worried about your future security. Sometimes, when fear or doubt kicks in, it helps to go back to basics and dot the i's and cross the t's. Deal with the facts, not the fantasy or fears.

Sunday 25th

You may be full of creative ideas today but unsure how to turn your ideas into reality. Allow yourself to dream as you enter the planning stage. This evening, focus on indulgent, calming rituals, like a hot bath or a big mug of hot chocolate with cream. Leave any worries behind you and get an early night.

Monday 26th

Volatile emotions could erupt first thing, whether you have an argument with your other half or someone at home triggers your mood. Try to deal with any issues swiftly rather than letting your feelings fester. Take yourself out of the drama zone and breathe in some fresh air.

Tuesday 27th

Be proactive at work today and make an effort to communicate and network with other people. It's a promising time for teamwork, especially if you know you're going to need some additional help on a project before long. Master your people skills and build some new connections.

Wednesday 28th

You may not have the best start to the day, but don't let it set you back. If things go wrong, get back on track quickly. You could achieve a lot today if you start communicating well and working alongside people of influence. Set feasible goals.

Thursday 29th

Concentrate on work whether you're in employment or looking for something new. Whatever your current situation, be thorough and consider your long-term goals. When you have something to work towards (like a savings plan or a new job), this can help to keep you focused and on track.

Friday 30th

The theme of steadiness continues. When you put your mind to your work and pay attention, you can get a lot done and make progress. It's a positive period to focus on your health and wellbeing and line up some fitness goals. Small, regular steps can lead to a big success.

JULY

. . . .

Saturday 1st

It's an excellent date for collaboration and persuasion, so loop your family into your goals. Float that exciting new idea again, or listen to what a relative has to say. You could achieve a lot at home and it's likely to be a joyful experience.

Sunday 2nd

Love could take you by surprise today but not necessarily in a good way. There's an unpredictable or erratic feel to your relationships. You might be the one who's questioning what you want, or maybe your other half is acting out of character. If this is the case, be patient.

Monday 3rd

Today's full moon is about looking at what works for you and what doesn't. Things to consider are your energy levels, how much you give to others and the work you do daily. Wherever in life you're flagging or feel low, this may highlight where change is required.

Tuesday 4th

There's a possibility that one form of work is coming to an end. If so, try to be accepting of what's happening and know that this period is about clearing things out so you can start afresh. Full moon energy is about letting go of unhelpful or stuck emotions.

Wednesday 5th

If you're caught up in a tricky relationship or partnership issue, either at work or in your private life, you should ideally do nothing today. Your work right now is personal, so turn your attention to yourself and your emotional wellbeing. Put yourself and your own needs first.

Thursday 6th

Today offers you an opportunity to confront someone in your life who's been behaving badly. It's not an easy day for relationships, but another person needs to understand what you will and won't put up with. This could relate to a personal or professional partnership.

Friday 7th

It's a good day for negotiation, whether that's your work contract or something in your personal life. You could use today's stars to rethink a gym membership. You may be surprised by what you're able to achieve now and a healthy discount or pay rise could be the reward.

Saturday 8th

Pay attention to your life admin and take your time with any major decisions. You could be full of good intentions to sort things out, but time and money could easily slip through your fingers. A charitable gesture is worth making.

Sunday 9th

There's a theme of karma around work and money; of reaping what you sow and being repaid for acts of kindness in your past. It's worth making sure you've planned for the future and reaching out to people to connect and network.

Monday 10th

Action planet Mars enters your joint finance zone today, so if you haven't already done so, now is very much the time to start thinking about money. This is your cue to pay close attention to your accounts and make sure you're up to date with everything over the next few weeks and months.

Tuesday 11th

There's a strong focus on your relationship and partnership zone. This could mean you find yourself up against competition or opposition as other people vie for the top spot. If this is the case, try not to let your emotions get the better of you and use logic and rationality to sort things out instead.

Wednesday 12th

Tune in during this midweek period and listen out for a conversation or interaction that brings new information your way. This could be in relation to the place you live, your family, your work or your health. Your stars feel unsettled but lively, and may bring the change you're craving.

Thursday 13th

You might have to use your clever brain to wiggle your way out of a tight spot today. If someone's on your back about something, their heavy-handed attitude won't win any favours. Insist on keeping things light and move quickly to ensure you stay one step ahead.

Friday 14th

You need the right people on your side, so turn to a partner in your life, either personal or professional. They could help to shed light on what's currently happening, and what you discover may prove to be a revelation for your work, your health, your home or your family.

Saturday 15th

You may be wistful if you know that you're soon going to be apart from your partner. This isn't necessarily a bad thing – after all, absence can make the heart grow fonder. However, if it's going to be a longer separation than you'd like, acknowledge your feelings. It's okay to be sad sometimes.

Sunday 16th

It's great when other people step in to help and offer you a new opportunity. This might be what happens now, and if so, the opportunity may be linked to your home and family. Anything that begins under lucky stars is likely to lead to success. Alternatively, today is a good day to declutter.

Monday 17th

Today's new moon highlights your work and health. It's a symbol of new beginnings but first, ask yourself where you might need to close the door to move on. There's a theme of sweeping out the old to create room for new energy to come flooding in.

Tuesday 18th

Your emotions are closely tied to what's happening in the life of your partner or a third party. Trust your intuition in knowing which path is the right one to take. You don't have to take immediate action now or do anything except listen to where your heart lies.

Wednesday 19th

This could be a powerful time for the partnerships in your life, both personal and professional. You could be deeply in love or starting a new business or joint venture. Notice who's in your life now and who you're teaming up with as there's dynamic and exciting energy here.

Thursday 20th

You may witness a comparison of different personalities and attitudes today. One individual is kindness personified and couldn't be more helpful, whether to you or someone close. On the other hand, another person could reveal their bullying nature, especially when it comes to money.

Friday 21st

You're right to be angry if someone is throwing their weight around and making unusually harsh demands in regard to a problem. Try not to stoop to their level and instead keep your anger at bay. Yes, you may have to work out a solution, but play for time if you can.

Saturday 22nd

There's profundity and depth to your current stars. You may have to confront any inner problems head-on, and you may not be able to avoid some level of soul-searching. Don't dismiss it, though, as it could be a healing or revelatory experience. Pay close attention to your job and your health.

Sunday 23rd

When it comes to love, it's important to talk; to look at what's working and what's not. This is the central theme of Venus retrograde in your relationship zone. Explore all your options and keep the lines of communication open. It's not the time to make a final decision on a relationship.

Monday 24th

During the coming month, the Sun is as far away from your star sign in the zodiac as it can be, so you may not feel full of energy or be the one in charge. Consider where in your life you may have to let other people step in and take the lead.

Tuesday 25th

You might be seeking an escape plan or be talking to your partner, either personal or professional, about a holiday, a trip or taking time away. If recent events have left you feeling shell-shocked, a break may be a good strategy to remove yourself from whatever's going on.

Wednesday 26th

Concentrate on your work and career, and consider where you're heading in life. The more you focus on your future path and your next steps, the more possibility opens up in front of you. Remind yourself today that everyone needs hope and faith in their lives.

Thursday 27th

You could reconnect with someone from your past today – possibly a lover, an ex or someone you used to work with. Either way, it's likely to be a heart-warming connection and you'll love hearing all about what's been happening in their lives. Reach out to other people.

Friday 28th

If you want to get a second opinion about something in your personal life, it's an excellent date to do so. A friend might not have the resources to help you right now, but you'll still enjoy a good chinwag. You might be up late this evening working out a plan and your next steps.

Saturday 29th

Put work and life admin to one side for today and line up some fun events. Friendship and group activities are well-starred, especially if there's a potential love interest joining in. Embrace fun and laughter, and remind yourself of all the things in life that lift your spirits.

Sunday 30th

If you want to ask for a raise or talk to someone about personal issues, this is a great day to work out what you're going to say or put in writing. Help could be at hand, whether you're asking for support or raising funds for charity. Ensure you put an important letter in the post.

Monday 31st

Start the week with a plan to deal with mundane matters and get back to basics. Follow up on a project, or if you want to move house, have a think about what you want out of a new home. It's an ideal day to work on your next steps, so get things down on paper and iron out the details.

AUGUST

Tuesday 1st
The full moon can be a time of clarity or insight when it comes to love and your close connections. Relationships are under the spotlight. Trust your intuition and know which relationships to pursue and where to back off.

Wednesday 2nd
When it comes to problems in your personal life, this isn't the time to go it alone. If you know you've got to have a difficult conversation, get advice from someone who knows you well. Your friends or family could provide a quick-fix solution to a financial issue.

Thursday 3rd
Mercury is the planet linked to facts and figures, communication and ideas. If you're gloomy about your current situation, don't keep things to yourself. Now's the time for order and structure, so seek help in areas that you need support in. Make a concrete plan to move forward.

Friday 4th
Current events could bring up stuff from your past or trigger emotions that have been buried or hidden. Ultimately, it's time to finalise the things you've been discussing this week and be firm with yourself and others. Put boundaries in place if someone has taken advantage of your good nature.

Saturday 5th

There are some weekends when you must put serious issues to one side and enjoy yourself. This is a day filled with feel-good vibes. Do what you're best at, make connections, meet up with friends and be part of your local community.

Sunday 6th

There are many kinds of love. As an Aquarius, you often know more about this than other people. Whether you're seeking friendship, desire or unconditional love, find the partnership that's right for you. Love doesn't always belong to one person – it can be shared.

Monday 7th

The feel-good vibe tips over into the working week. You could find that everyday matters and chores go out of the window today – you have more important activities to be getting on with. There may be someone in your life who knows how to put a big smile on your face.

Tuesday 8th

If you have an entrepreneurial nature, today might be a good time to consider a new venture, possibly to do with home and family matters. There are good opportunities in this area today!

Wednesday 9th

Try not to read too much into a loved one's behaviour. Love planet Venus remains retrograde for the next few weeks, which can often be a time when the truth is hidden. Misunderstandings could happen and both parties involved may change their mind more than once.

Thursday 10th

Respond to good news this morning and you could bring an important matter to completion. This may trigger an emotional response, especially if you're cutting ties with, or letting go of, someone or something that's played an important role in your life. Freedom beckons.

Friday 11th

The weekend could start early as you're more interested in love, socialising and having fun than work and chores. You may be ready to put a financial issue to one side and turn your attention to the things you love in life. It's not wise to go wild, but that might not stop you.

Saturday 12th

It won't be the most exciting of days if you're at work, but the idea of earning extra money will see you through. Pay close attention now to your health and fitness. You could start the day with a workout or jog. Invest in your wellbeing.

Sunday 13th

Your astrology today looks gorgeous, with your stars promising good fortune for close connections. Someone might return to your life to help you, or you could engage with your partner or someone close on a deeper level. It could be a passionate union.

Monday 14th

A lot is going on in your opposite star sign this week, which might mean that you're not the one in control in some area of your life; when planets are in Leo, you are at the mercy of other people. Alternatively, other people may gift you with their brilliance. It can work both ways!

Tuesday 15th

This may be a time when partnerships are more dominant in your life, both personally and professionally. Notice who comes into your life and the people you're drawn towards this week. When you get the right people on your side, magic can happen.

Wednesday 16th

Today's new moon is the ideal time to reassess your one-to-ones as new information comes to light. Decide where your heart lies and set some new intentions around love and partnership. Be with the people who lift you up rather than bringing you down.

Thursday 17th

Look for an escape route today. Some quick-thinking and rapid research could help you find a loophole or a way out of a financial issue that's tied you up or held you back for some time. It is important to have a long-term money plan.

. . . .

Friday 18th

We're heading into the Mercury retrograde phase in a few days. It's important to focus on money matters sooner rather than later as they could impede your financial progress in some way. Today is great for correspondence, conversations and negotiations. Get talking.

Saturday 19th

The emphasis on your finances continues into the weekend. Rather than feeling frustrated or getting angry about a money issue, now's the time to take action instead of hoping everything sorts itself out. Sex is under the cosmic spotlight too, and your fantasy life could be fizzing.

Sunday 20th

It's a good day to book a holiday or sign up for a course of study. The key areas of travel and education will be getting a lot of stimulation over the next few months. You're wise to sign and seal a contract before Mercury switches direction in three days.

Monday 21st

You'll enjoy yourself more if you go on holiday or a study course. Get together with a partner or good friend if you're seeking adventure and new experiences. You'll undoubtedly meet people when you're there, but the journey will be more fun with a companion.

Tuesday 22nd

Today's planetary influence is seductive and inspirational, but potentially misleading and emotional, too. If this is the case, keep a firm grip on reality and don't let anyone else persuade you otherwise. Don't believe everything you hear, as some people are not to be trusted.

Wednesday 23rd

There's less emphasis on your close relationships from today. However, that's not to say that love's gone quiet; in fact, it's the opposite. There may be plenty of opportunities for you to enjoy your one-to-ones and maximise your close connections, both personal and professional.

Thursday 24th

Mercury turns retrograde, which is potentially tricky for money. If you are experiencing financial issues, proceed cautiously over the next three weeks. This phase is helpful if you want to delve deeper into money matters, but put off any major investments or important decisions for now.

Friday 25th

This could be a soul-searching time for you, and you might be diving deep into taboo areas such as money, power, sex, death and rebirth. This is not the time to avoid any personal or relationship issues. Say it like it is and don't sidestep the important stuff.

Saturday 26th

You could be weighing up two different options: either you're going to do the sensible thing and not spend any money, or you're going to splurge on a new adventure as you know it may do you the world of good. Ideally, find a way to do both by making a strategic compromise.

Sunday 27th

If things have become a bit too intense lately, book a last-minute trip away and take some much-deserved time out. Being somewhere different can help you shift your perspective and see life from a fresh angle.

Monday 28th

You may get sidetracked today if there's excitement at home or within your family. Alternatively, you may be required to change plans fast to help someone out. From mid-afternoon onwards, when the Moon is in Aquarius, turn your attention to your plans and what's next for you.

Tuesday 29th

Today's stars could bring the unexpected when events happen quickly. You may be going back to the past or revisiting future plans. It's a good time to be spontaneous, do something last minute and vary your routine. It doesn't benefit you for things to remain the same.

Wednesday 30th

If you're typical of your star sign, you have a stubborn nature and usually think that you're right and the other person's wrong. You might also be wild, erratic and on the edge. You may experience both today in any order.

Thursday 31st

You may be feeling overly emotional during today's full moon, especially where money's concerned. If you need to make a big decision about your life, you should ideally wait until the middle of next month, when you can be surer of your position.

SEPTEMBER
....

Friday 1st

It's potentially a tense day emotionally and you might want to let off steam. If so, go for a long walk after work or book a session in the gym. You might not have much willpower around money today.

Saturday 2nd

Love and relationships are about to reach a significant turning point, so it's a good time to meet up with someone close and have a heart-to-heart. It might seem as if you're talking about the same issues and going over old ground, but it's worth it if you're able to reconnect.

Sunday 3rd

If you're not engaging the activist side of your nature, why not? Your star sign is the most humanitarian of all the zodiac, and you're at your best when you're involved in your community or actively engaged with social or environmental issues. Be true to who you are.

Monday 4th

If you're in a relationship or marriage, this is an ideal date for a heart-to-heart or to try to sort out an ongoing issue. It's a good day to declare your love and intentions around partnership. You could also experience a lucky break because of someone else's support.

. . . .

Tuesday 5th

You might have to let go of a home or family goal for a short while. You may not have the means to act on it right now, or you might just know it's not the right time to act on your wishes. You could reconsider your position at the end of the year.

Wednesday 6th

Create a business plan, track your budget and get on top of your life admin. Make a point of dealing with anything you've been avoiding and confront any issues head-on. You're wise to be cautious rather than overly extravagant.

Thursday 7th

There are some days when all you want to do is let your hair down, go wild and forget about the serious side of life. Today could easily be one of those days, especially if you've grown disillusioned or dissatisfied with your current situation. Kick back and take it easy.

Friday 8th

The flow of money, goodwill or abundance could indicate a windfall, a cash bonus, a gift or a return on investment. Be generous. Make a decision on something today that might positively affect your future.

Saturday 9th

It's a good time to focus on your domestic situation, your home and family. You might be undertaking a major clear out, have roped your family into decorating, or be gathering the clans. Alternatively, you could decide to work this weekend and boost your cash flow in the process.

Sunday 10th

Your devotion to work and domestic matters is admirable, but don't forget that this is the day of rest and a chance to prioritise self-care. Pay attention to any aches and pains before they turn into something more serious – prevention is better than cure.

Monday 11th

What you may be seeking is a soulmate connection rather than a fun playmate. This is a period in your life when you could experience deep and intense emotions and want more than a superficial hook-up. A relationship that began in early June could be flourishing beautifully.

Tuesday 12th

Take a close look at what's motivating you, especially when it comes to love and relationships. If you're typical of your star sign, there's a side of your nature that appreciates freedom and the single life. Notice when this need gets in the way of a more loving committed partnership.

Wednesday 13th

Earth-sign energy dominates now. The earth element is slow-moving, predictable and routine. This doesn't always suit your airy nature, but you can learn a lot when you adopt a slow and steady approach to life. Take advice from your earth-sign friends, Taurus, Virgo and Capricorn.

Thursday 14th

There may be a turning point today concerning an important issue. If you play your cards right, you could work out an agreement that not only suits you but ensures your future security. A great opportunity could arise when you dare to risk.

Friday 15th

There's not only a new moon tonight, which is a symbol of new beginnings, but Mercury turns direct. Two turning points, two green lights – take quick action to boost your prospects. You can't rule out a financial victory today.

Saturday 16th

If things are difficult with someone you see a lot, take a step back. Arguments could flare quickly, which won't be helpful to either of you in the long run. It's a great day to be spontaneous and try something new. For you, this is linked to events concerning your home and your family.

Sunday 17th

There's less of a rebellious edge to your stars today, but this doesn't necessarily mean you should take the sensible path. In fact, with two of the best planets on your side, there may be a good opportunity available for you to take a risk and do more of what you love.

Monday 18th

Today, your stars hint at security, so take care of the essentials of life. Look at new ways of creating firm foundations for yourself and the ones you love. Consider whether you're ready to take on a more responsible role at work or home.

Tuesday 19th

There's a cosmic heads-up today to stay as conscious as you can around money and spending. While a little indulgence is good for the soul, you're wise not to overdo it. If you can't afford to pay for the thing you want, put it out of your mind and focus your attention elsewhere.

Wednesday 20th

It's worth putting in some extra effort today to complete a
job or work-related project. You'll feel a sense of achievement
if you meet your deadline or fulfil a promise. It might mean
you're too exhausted later on to join in with a social event, but
the results will be worth it.

Thursday 21st

It would be a good time to consider all your options in terms of
planning for the future. Lean on family or someone from your
past for help or support. Your willpower is strong now, so use
it to your benefit.

Friday 22nd

You may be forgetful today, so double check you haven't
missed a friend's birthday. You can sometimes get too caught
up with technology and lose track of the outside world. It's
not like you, but you might want to swap a big night out for a
quiet night in – it could do you the world of good.

Saturday 23rd

The Sun's move from an earth sign to an air sign is good news
for you. The focus turns towards travel and wide-open spaces,
life experience and learning. It would be an ideal time to take
yourself off somewhere different or line up a trip for 2024.

Sunday 24th

Start your day peacefully with some affirmation or meditation
practice. It's an ideal date to nurture your spiritual path or
seek one to include in your daily rituals. Focus on your beliefs
and your philosophy on life; take yourself away from the ego
and into the world. Seek its meaning.

Monday 25th

Return to a conversation you had back in August. There's a theme of second chances or something coming full circle and reaching completion – possibly in relation to a home or family issue. A lunchtime date could yield good news.

Tuesday 26th

Stand your ground if someone close to you is behaving erratically or acting out of character. You might have to let them know that you're there for them and you're going nowhere. If you're the one who feels restless, make sure this doesn't impact detrimentally on a close relationship.

Wednesday 27th

Keep firm boundaries in place when it comes to money. Ensure you value your skills and don't undersell yourself; your self-worth is directly linked to success at the moment. It's a good idea to stay up late if you're planning a move and want to research property.

Thursday 28th

Be aware that any ideas or plans you come up with today could be unrealistic. If in doubt, pay attention to the facts and stick to the figures. It may not help to talk to another person either, as they're likely to baffle or confuse you more. Let things be for now.

Friday 29th

Today's full moon highlights travel options and study activities. Think about how you can expand your life experience, not only physically, but mentally and spiritually as well. You might have to say no to one opportunity so that you can say yes to something better.

Saturday 30th

Keep the lines of communication open, especially if you want more information regarding a travel project or study idea. Talk to someone in your family or an expert. A spontaneous conversation could prove illuminating.

OCTOBER

· · · · · · · · · · · · · · · · ·

Sunday 1st

Your current astrology suggests benefitting from a duvet day, so it's an ideal date to chill out and indulge in comfort. Alternatively, spend the day in nature, whether in the garden, allotment or on a walk. Switch off the news and social media to rest and restore your energy levels.

Monday 2nd

It's a day when people are entranced by hype and seduction, yourself included. You could read or hear news or information that sounds like a quick fix, but any deal is probably too good to be true without digging a little deeper.

Tuesday 3rd

This is not the time to avoid a problem in your life, so say it like it is and don't sidestep the important stuff. Nail down the details, face reality and get down to the nitty-gritty. Once you've explored all the options, then you can act decisively.

Wednesday 4th

Both the Sun and Moon are in your element today, so you're likely to feel more balanced and harmonious in your energy levels. Do whatever you need to ensure the scales of life are tipped in the right direction, and focus on good times, exploration and new projects.

Thursday 5th

There's a welcome shift today as you say goodbye to a tricky chapter of your life. You might have been exploring the murkier and scarier areas of your psyche. As a welcome antidote, turn your gaze outwards into life.

Friday 6th

If you want to get your work done quickly, ask for help from other people. If you're at home, this might be your family or a neighbour. If you're in the office, appeal to the generosity of a team member. Wherever you are, this is a day to foster close relationships.

Saturday 7th

You may find out today that travel or study plans aren't going to work out. One reason why you might not be able to get away imminently is because of what's going on at work. If this is true for you, wait for better timing. It is coming.

Sunday 8th

Your stars today could flag up conflict with someone you meet or someone from your past. This could be a spontaneous encounter, or you might be drawn back towards someone you've known for a long time. Trust your gut: if it feels wrong, don't go there.

Monday 9th

Personal issues and your inner thoughts and feelings are in the foreground. Steer clear of conflict or tension and don't get involved in other people's arguments. If you're aware that a relationship must adapt to survive, decide what this means for you and whether you're ready to take the next step.

Tuesday 10th

It's the right time to turn your attention towards a personal or professional partnership. Something is coming to an end, whether it's time to move on and say goodbye or there are new practicalities to consider. You may miss someone who's not around as much as they used to be.

Wednesday 11th

You might require some time out today to focus on your inner life and emotions, especially if things feel intense. You're wise to consider your self-worth and your future path. Make concrete plans to firm up your reserves and strengthen your foundations.

Thursday 12th

You're wise to get things moving when it comes to your career and vocational path. Stop procrastinating and be confident and bold in your next moves. This would be a good time to apply for a job, chase up a promotion or explore new work and career options.

Friday 13th

The focus remains on your working life. You may notice your drive and get-up-and-go returns. This might have something to do with the fact that you're ready to get organised and on top of any life admin. Get your ambitious juices flowing and set some goals for the next few months.

Saturday 14th

Any kind of coaching or guidance could help you gain insight today. Be open to learning and experiment with new beliefs and ideas. Today's solar eclipse suggests that new beginnings will open up for you once you let go of a dream or goal that's not working out.

Sunday 15th

It's time to put your money where your mouth is. If you want to change your career, set up a business or find a new job then channel your energy and ambition accordingly. Don't let anyone or anything hold you back from achieving your long-held goals.

Monday 16th

You may have to change plans today and tomorrow if work comes in or you're committed to pursuing your next steps. Someone at home or in the family could be very persuasive and try to change your mind, but stay on track with what's most important to you.

Tuesday 17th

If you know you have some big decisions to make when it comes to your future path, find time to daydream and visualise what's coming next. This can help prepare you and get you ready to embrace change, rather than trying to resist it. Cancel a social engagement if it helps.

Wednesday 18th

If you have friends in your life who are a bad influence, be wary of invitations from them over the next couple of days. If you're typical of your star sign, you don't like to decline social fun and games, but you do have to consider how serious you are about your progression in work.

Thursday 19th

The temptation to slack off your goals could come your way later on today. Remind yourself of the reasons why you're working hard or chasing success. Engage your emotions in whatever you're doing and it will be easier to stay focused.

Friday 20th

If you are starting a new project or seeking employment, pay close attention to the details. It's an excellent date to schedule an important meeting or interview, or to sit an exam. If you're busy with travel or study plans, it's best to keep your options open for a while.

Saturday 21st

Try not to get too upset if plans don't work out this weekend. Be willing to take a step back and reconsider your options. Your current stars suggest that you may have to say no to one opportunity so that you can say yes to something else better that materialises.

Sunday 22nd

Don't fall into negative thinking or let fear control you. Keep your eyes firmly fixed on your future goals and play the long game. It may be a Sunday, but try to arrange a meeting or interview for the week ahead and consider what's next and where you're heading.

Monday 23rd

The key to work and career success is to do what you love and what you're passionate about. This isn't about the hard slog; it's about utilising your skills and talents and honing your natural abilities. Today's stars add commitment and intensity to your work ambitions.

Tuesday 24th

Focus your attention and channel your drive and energy into a work-related project or your future path. If you want a promotion, go for it; if you're looking for a new job or contract, get serious about it. The planets are lining up in the most ambitious zone of your horoscope.

Wednesday 25th

It's a positive week to use your connections. Make the right alliances and get good people on your side. It's not only about what you know but who you know this week, so balance the two. There may be exciting news for someone close, and their success could benefit you in return.

Thursday 26th

It may be time to put sleepless nights behind you and look at constructive ways of dealing with any anxiety or worries. Today is potentially brilliant for all forms of communication, so reach out to other people. Make new contacts, gather vital information and keep moving forward.

Friday 27th

Life is speeding up and may require a gear shift. It's a good day for ideas, brainstorming and making new connections. Leap into action fast and don't hang around if there's someone you want to talk to or interact with. You might find that you have plenty to talk about.

Saturday 28th

The past and future could clash during the eclipse. You may see where you've come from and where you're heading to. You might be juggling home and work or be pulled between the two. This tension is at its height but trust your instincts in knowing which path to follow.

Sunday 29th

Think on your feet and don't rely too heavily on other people. Talk planet Mercury is active this eclipse weekend and is a rational and logical influence. Action planet Mars is also involved. Both planets together are urging you to walk your walk and talk your talk.

Monday 30th

You might have to let go of something to start over – perhaps your private life in favour of your public life. Maybe you know it's time to let go of old beliefs that hold you back. The more you engage with your personal development, the faster you progress.

Tuesday 31st

Things could feel intense at the moment. Perhaps you're so caught up with work and life admin that you have little time for anything or anyone else. That could change today as someone's spontaneous invitation puts a smile on your face. Say yes.

NOVEMBER

. . . .

Wednesday 1st

Try not to listen to other people's opinions if this muddies the waters and confuses your thinking. Be objective and rational in making a major decision and you won't go far wrong. Make progress with your goals and aims and know that this is your chance to be seen in a positive light.

Thursday 2nd

There's an easy flow in your stars today, so make the most of it. Once you find your flow, you can accomplish work or a domestic project easily and smoothly. It's wise to get on with things today as the weekend's events could prove disruptive.

Friday 3rd

Try not to let money slip through your fingers and ensure you pin other people down if they're being elusive. Also, don't entrust an important project to a third party to deal with without first checking their credentials. This includes a family member as well.

Saturday 4th

Patience could be in short supply today. Be careful what you say and try not to act impulsively or promise too much. It could be easy to air your thoughts when you might be better off keeping them to yourself. You may have to revise your plans if changes take place unexpectedly.

Sunday 5th

A compromise may have to be found if you're to keep everyone happy. When you're in a busy work patch or keen to progress your plans, this means you have less time for the ones you love. Don't tip the scales too far in either direction – find a healthy work/life balance.

Monday 6th

It could be a disruptive start to the working week, whether childcare plans fall through or you have to drop everything to be there for a member of your family. Take a step back from a close relationship if things have become too intense. The week will get better as it goes on.

Tuesday 7th

If you are aware of your dreams, now would be an excellent time to write a dream journal. Your creative ideas might filter into your conscious mind and guide you in a new direction. Share your hopes and dreams with your family. Alternatively, reach out to someone and lend a helping hand.

Wednesday 8th

There's a welcome breath of fresh air today and your stars are encouraging you to pursue the bigger picture in life. You may be back in your favourite place. Immerse yourself in a course of study, or plan a trip. Love and foreign connections are linked.

Thursday 9th

If you were up late last night unable to stop thinking about work or plans, aim to take it easy today. If you can't stop thinking about someone, it could be a sign to get in touch with them. If you met this person while you were travelling or studying, your instincts are likely to be spot on.

Friday 10th

Start prioritising your friends today and make plans to catch up. Admittedly, a lack of cash could stop you from joining in with everything, but don't let that put you off reaching out and connecting with your loved ones. Some down time and outrageous fun is called for.

Saturday 11th

There could be an issue at the office or with your home and family situation. You may be feeling rebellious this weekend, but take a deep breath before acting impulsively and don't take any unnecessary risks. This is especially important if you're out and about tonight.

Sunday 12th

This is the dark phase of the moon, the time to rest and recharge your batteries. Tomorrow's new moon promises new beginnings but for now, things are hidden. Let family persuade you to spend time with them and enjoy a day where you chill out, kick back and do little else.

Monday 13th

What you put in place on or around today's new moon could help you launch a new project. You may discover that the seeds you've sown over the past few weeks finally bear fruit, or you might feel ready to change what you're doing, embrace freedom and move on.

Tuesday 14th

Take yourself away from your work today if you can. This is especially important if the rug was pulled out from under you yesterday and you didn't get the backing or support that you expected. A welcome antidote to any work stress is the company of good friends.

Wednesday 15th

Catch up with a good friend, perhaps at lunchtime, and the two of you can put the world to rights. You might be talking about philosophical issues or the state of the world. Alternatively, you could be planning a holiday or a fun trip together. Line up something new to look forward to.

Thursday 16th

Your thoughts may turn to your inner concerns, a private or personal issue. You may not be feeling hugely confident, but someone in your family could be your biggest cheerleader. If you want a boost to your spirits, reach out to the person who knows how to make you smile.

Friday 17th

It's always positive to have hopes and wishes in life and goals to aim for. The planet that represents dreams is powerful today and can help you visualise your next steps. Alternatively, find the coach or mentor who's right for you and has a reputation of aiming high.

Saturday 18th

Intensity and ambition are in your stars today. You might be angry about what's happening, which fires you up and gets you motivated. You could be passionate about a current project you're involved in. Either way, it's a day of full-on attack and excitement.

Sunday 19th

Have a day to yourself, or at least ensure that whatever you're involved in is what you want to do. You might join in with a group of people in the name of a good cause. You could be planning your next holiday or trip away. Use your day off to boost your spirits.

Monday 20th

Scorpio is the sign of transformation, of seeking out hidden riches and digging deep to find the gold in life. Scorpio season is an indication that change needs to take place on an inner level before you can see change out in the world. Bear this in mind moving forward.

Tuesday 21st

The planets are completing their journey through your career and future zone. Now might be the right time to call it a day concerning a project or job that you've outgrown. Alternatively, you could be pushing hard to reach an imminent deadline. Give it your best shot.

Wednesday 22nd

The Sun moves into your friendship and group zone today. This is where you can rediscover enthusiasm and inspiration, and it's through other people in your life that you connect to your energy and passion. Extend your network and make new connections.

Thursday 23rd

You seem to have a different attitude towards money these days. Instead of putting cash on credit and paying it off later, you may choose to find the money or save up to pay your way. You may not like telling someone you can't afford to join their plans, but needs must.

Friday 24th

It's a positive week to meet new people, whether you're seeking friends online or you want to get to know people close to where you live. Be friendly and sociable, as the benefits to you are worth it. You may discover that your activist tendencies are back and raring to go.

Saturday 25th

Financial constraints are never easy to deal with. If you're the one under stress, keep thinking of the bigger picture and remember that it should all be worth it. If a friend's struggling, make time for them to show your support. A moment of synchronicity or a memory could stir your thoughts.

Sunday 26th

The full moon currently shining brightly in the night sky promises a good day to catch up with friends and prioritise fun and socialising. Get out and about and enjoy yourself. This is even more important if there's a sniff of romance on the horizon.

Monday 27th

The current full moon phase could coincide with a big event or drama in a friend's life. Your friends are important to you, so you'll want to show solidarity. If someone's struggling, don't leave them hanging but talk to them. Show your support and help them move forward.

Tuesday 28th

You could choose to go to a social event on your own without your other half. Alternatively, perhaps it's time to knock an illicit relationship or unrequited love on the head. Today's stars may bring matters to light that require your close attention in affairs of the heart.

Wednesday 29th

If you haven't got a lot done so far this week, here's your opportunity to get busy and be productive. It's a day to get your head down and focus on the task at hand. If you've bills to pay or payday's coming, this is your incentive to concentrate and get things done.

Thursday 30th

There may be nothing stopping you at work or concerning your fitness. Whatever your personal goal, you have a clear run to tick off your to-do list and achieve your aims. Reward yourself this evening with a film or an impromptu dinner invitation.

DECEMBER

. . . .

Friday 1st

If you can, create some time for yourself over the next few weeks. Your astrology highlights the need for rest and retreat, alongside some social and fun times. Learn to take it easy, quieten your mind and do the inner work ready for 2024 and new beginnings.

Saturday 2nd

If your life's been lacking direction, now's the time to reorient your compass and get back on track with your long-term goals and aims. It's a good idea to step things up a notch and decide where you can make your mark within society. Add a sensitive touch to your ambition.

Sunday 3rd

You may be missing someone in your life, whether they've gone abroad or they're studying away from home. It's sometimes easy for you to cut off from what you're feeling, but turn your attention to your close relationships, especially if you know you've been avoiding your emotions.

Monday 4th

Love planet Venus moves into your career and future zone today. This flags up the possibility of a love affair at work or a secret flirtation over the next few weeks. However, it also suggests teaming up with people at work, which could make everyone's job easier.

Tuesday 5th

The theme at work is collaboration. Align yourself with the right people and you can go far. Look out for a role model or someone who can help you make progress in your chosen career or vocation. A woman in a position of influence could help open doors for you.

Wednesday 6th

Don't be tempted to cave in today if there's something you want to buy or invest in, especially if you've been putting in a lot of hard work to turn your finances around. Whatever's on offer could look like a great idea, but beware the hype.

Thursday 7th

There's a whiff of adventure in the air today, especially if you're talking to a friend who lives abroad. It's a good time to pursue social activities, so you might line up a holiday or weekend away. You may even be considering a move abroad next year.

Friday 8th

Make time for someone in your family today or discuss your plans for the festive period. If you're seeking inspiration, reach out to other people as one conversation could give you exactly what you're looking for.

Saturday 9th

It may be the weekend, but your stars look lively for your career and vocation, as well as your next steps in life. This may be due to someone you meet this weekend when you're out and about socially. You might envy their career or life path, which could give you food for thought.

Sunday 10th

If you spend the day lying around at home, you may end up feeling restless and wanting more from life. It might be a good idea to line up something fun and inspirational and be around people who stir your ambition. Love and business are closely aligned, whatever this means for you.

Monday 11th

Start the week as you mean to go on. If you know you're going to be busy on the run-up to Christmas, get organised and plan ahead. If you want to talk to someone about your career path or you're seeking ideas on what to study next, arrange a social get-together this evening.

Tuesday 12th

Today's new moon highlights your hopes and wishes, so it's an excellent time to think ahead, plan your next steps and fire some arrows into the sky to see where they land. There's a fun, social vibe to this new moon, which is good news if you're out this evening.

Wednesday 13th

Today's Mercury retrograde phase may see you diving deep into hidden places. What's going on behind the scenes is as important as what's visible. Listen to your inner voice and try not to dismiss unconscious thoughts. Calm your busy mind through rest and retreat.

Thursday 14th

Your best strategy is to slow down today. If you're at work, take the pace slow. If you're at home, do whatever helps you rest and relax – cooking, crafts, meditation or a soak in the bath. When you quieten your mind, you can find the answers you're seeking.

Friday 15th

If you're too busy or stressed out, be strict with your schedule and cancel anything unnecessary. If you're burning the candle at both ends, even more reason to prioritise some time out. If you're typical of your star sign, you like to work hard and play hard.

Saturday 16th

Turn your attention towards yourself and your needs. It's a good time to aim for inner calm and do more of what feeds you and nurtures you. This might mean delegating some of your to-do list to another person who may be happy to help. Catch up with good friends this evening.

Sunday 17th

You may be in a giving mood, which is great if you have the money to spare, though you might be offering compassion and kindness instead. Do be wary of being seduced or deceived when it comes to money, however, and keep close tabs on what's going out and coming in.

Monday 18th

Keep talking to members of your family if you can't agree on what's happening over the festive period. There may be one person in your life who requires extra support now. If so, find the time to be there for them. Sometimes, all it takes is to pick up the phone.

Tuesday 19th

It all depends today on how much you trust your intuition. Ideally, you want to do what feels right rather than what you think is right. However, if money is involved then you mustn't fool yourself. Take advice from someone you trust and double-check your motivations.

Wednesday 20th

Action speaks louder than words today. Get things done rather than worrying about what other people think. It's important to remind yourself that good enough is better than being a perfectionist. When it comes to love, you may decide to pull back from a flirtatious liaison.

Thursday 21st

This isn't a good date to get on the wrong side of someone in a position of power. You may not agree with their way of doing things, but right now your best strategy is to say less not more. Rein in your impulsive tendencies.

Friday 22nd

You can benefit from some time alone this weekend. The most important conversation you have now is with yourself, whether you're seeking reassurance, self-love or inspiration. Turn your attention inwards and focus on me-time ahead of the next few days.

Saturday 23rd

You may hear from an old friend unexpectedly – perhaps someone from your past, or a friend who's gone quiet on you. It may take a while to get back to how things were before but it's a good date to start talking. If someone in your family is unlucky in love, be there for them.

Sunday 24th

You have a reputation for being a social superstar but today you may choose to show the world how wise and responsible you are. This might mean playing the dutiful parent or child, going on a silent retreat, or saying no to the Christmas Eve party. Do what works for you.

Monday 25th

Happy Christmas! There's a social vibe to the big day itself, and you'll enjoy seeing the looks on the faces of your loved ones as they open their presents. You'll be the one joining in with all the fun games, telling jokes and having a laugh.

Tuesday 26th

There's a slightly argumentative edge to today's stars, so choose your Boxing Day companions carefully. Keep the atmosphere light and hold back on discussing serious issues if this could end up in a row. Your thoughts may turn to a romantic moment you had earlier in the month.

Wednesday 27th

During today's full moon, you may recognise that giving means more than extravagant gifts as the humanitarian side of your nature is called forth. What you do for other people is more worthwhile than any expensive gesture over the festive period. You might consider volunteering.

Thursday 28th

It could be lively if you're catching up with friends or you're busy with a group, club or society. A sporting event might be in your diary. If you get on well with the people you're with, expect some boisterous antics, but be wary it doesn't turn nasty.

Friday 29th

If you want to join a new group or you hear about a social occasion that sounds right up your street, ask for an invitation or introduction and expand your network. If you've fallen out with someone recently, this evening is the ideal time to make amends, to kiss and make up.

Saturday 30th

Love and friendship are linked over the next few weeks. You're wise to keep talking and get to know someone better before leaping in feet first. The turning point comes in the next couple of days. If you're in a relationship or married, make today a date day.

Sunday 31st

It's a wonderful New Year's Eve to spend time with your family or take a trip down memory lane. Return to the place you grew up or reconnect with someone from your past. Set some new intentions around your home, especially if you're looking to move in the coming year.

Aquarius

....

PEOPLE WHO SHARE
YOUR SIGN

PEOPLE WHO SHARE YOUR SIGN

. . . .

Born to be different and shake things up, Aquarians are the liberating air sign that are prepared to ruffle some feathers if needed. From the speeches of Abraham Lincoln to the words of Virginia Woolf, the unique insight and intellect that so many Aquarians have make them a sign to listen to and to take notice of. Discover which of these Aquarians share your birthday and see if you can spot the similarities.

21st January

BooBoo Stewart (1994), Jerry Trainor (1977), Emma Bunton (1976), Geena Davis (1956), Paul Allen (1953), Billy Ocean (1950), Benny Hill (1924), Christian Dior (1905), Grigori Rasputin (1869)

22nd January

Logic (1990), Hidetoshi Nakata (1977), Gabriel Macht (1972), Guy Fieri (1968), Diane Lane (1965), Linda Blair (1959), Steve Perry (1949), John Hurt (1940)

23rd January

Doutzen Kroes (1985), Draya Michele (1985), Arjen Robben (1984), Tiffani Thiessen (1974), Mariska Hargitay (1964), Princess Caroline of Hanover (1957), Richard Dean Anderson (1950), Édouard Manet (1832)

24th January
Luis Suárez (1987), Mischa Barton (1986), Justin Baldoni (1984), Frankie Grande (1983), Tatyana Ali (1979), Kristen Schaal (1978), Ed Helms (1974), Kenya Moore (1971), Sharon Tate (1943)

25th January
Calum Hood (1996), Alicia Keys (1981), Xavi (1980), Princess Charlene of Monaco (1978), Virginia Woolf (1882)

26th January
Colin O'Donoghue (1981), Brendan Rodgers (1973), José Mourinho (1963), Wayne Gretzky (1961), Eddie Van Halen (1955), Angela Davis (1944), Paul Newman (1925), Louis Zamperini (1917), Maria von Trapp (1905)

27th January
Rosamund Pike (1979), Patton Oswalt (1969), Alan Cumming (1965), Bridget Fonda (1964), Narciso Rodriguez (1961), Mimi Rogers (1956), Mikhail Baryshnikov (1948), Beatrice Tinsley (1941), Lewis Carroll (1832)

28th January
Ariel Winter (1998), Will Poulter (1993), J. Cole (1985), Elijah Wood (1981), Nick Carter (1980), Gianluigi Buffon (1978), Rick Ross (1976), Carlos Slim (1940), Alan Alda (1936)

29th January
Adam Lambert (1982), Sara Gilbert (1975), Heather Graham (1970), Oprah Winfrey (1954), Tom Selleck (1945), Katharine Ross (1940), Anton Chekhov (1860)

30th January

Eiza González (1990), Wilmer Valderrama (1980), Christian Bale (1974), Phil Collins (1951), Dick Cheney, U.S. Vice President (1941), Franklin D. Roosevelt, U.S. President (1882)

31st January

Amy Jackson (1992), Marcus Mumford (1987), Justin Timberlake (1981), Kerry Washington (1977), Portia de Rossi (1973), Minnie Driver (1970), Daniel Moder (1969), Jonathan Banks (1947), Carol Channing (1921), Jackie Robinson (1919), Baba Vanga (1911)

1st February

Harry Styles (1994), Heather Morris (1987), Ronda Rousey (1987), Lauren Conrad (1986), Abbi Jacobson (1984), Michael C. Hall (1971), Lisa Marie Presley (1968), Princess Stéphanie of Monaco (1965), Langston Hughes (1902)

2nd February

Gerard Piqué (1987), Gemma Arterton (1986), Gemma Collins (1981), Christine Bleakley (1979), Shakira (1977), Christie Brinkley (1954), Duncan Bannatyne (1949), Farrah Fawcett (1947), David Jason (1940), Ayn Rand (1905), James Joyce (1882)

3rd February

Sean Kingston (1990), Amal Clooney (1978), Isla Fisher (1976), Warwick Davis (1970), Maura Tierney (1965), Joachim Löw (1960), Nathan Lane (1956), Blythe Danner (1943), Norman Rockwell (1894)

4th February
Hannibal Buress (1983), Gavin DeGraw (1977), Cam'ron (1976), Natalie Imbruglia (1975), Oscar De La Hoya (1973), Alice Cooper (1948), Rosa Parks (1913)

5th February
Neymar (1992), Darren Criss (1987), Cristiano Ronaldo (1985), Carlos Tevez (1984), Tiwa Savage (1980), Tim Meadows (1961), Michael Sheen (1969), Laura Linney (1964), Duff McKagan (1964), Jennifer Jason Leigh (1962)

6th February
Tinashe (1993), Dane DeHaan (1986), Alice Eve (1982), Rick Astley (1966), Kathy Najimy (1957), Bob Marley (1945), Ronald Reagan, U.S. President (1911), Babe Ruth (1895)

7th February
Bea Miller (1999), Jacksepticeye (1990), Deborah Ann Woll (1985), Ashton Kutcher (1978), Chris Rock (1965), Garth Brooks (1962), Eddie Izzard (1962), James Spader (1960), Laura Ingalls Wilder (1876), Charles Dickens (1812)

8th February
Klay Thompson (1990), Seth Green (1974), Mauricio Macri (1959), Mary Steenburgen (1953), John Williams (1932), James Dean (1931), Dmitri Mendeleev (1834), Jules Verne (1828)

9th February

Michael B. Jordan (1987), Rose Leslie (1987), Tom Hiddleston (1981), Zhang Ziyi (1979), Charlie Day (1976), Amber Valletta (1974), Chris Gardner (1954), Joe Pesci (1943), Carole King (1942)

10th February

Chloë Grace Moretz (1997), Emma Roberts (1991), Radamel Falcao (1986), Uzo Aduba (1981), Stephanie Beatriz (1981), Holly Willoughby (1981), Don Omar (1978), Elizabeth Banks (1974), Laura Dern (1967), Bertolt Brecht (1898)

11th February

Taylor Lautner (1992), Natalie Dormer (1982), Kelly Rowland (1981), Damian Lewis (1971), Jennifer Aniston (1969), Sheryl Crow (1962), Burt Reynolds (1936), Leslie Nielsen (1926), Thomas Edison (1847)

12th February

Mike Posner (1988), Iko Uwais (1983), Christina Ricci (1980), Naseem Hamed (1974), Josh Brolin (1968), Chris McCandless (1968), Charles Darwin (1809), Abraham Lincoln, U.S. President (1809)

13th February

Memphis Depay (1994), Mena Suvari (1979), Robbie Williams (1974), Kelly Hu (1968), Peter Gabriel (1950), Jerry Springer (1944), Kim Novak (1933)

14th February

Freddie Highmore (1992), Ángel Di María (1988), Edinson
Cavani (1987), Danai Gurira (1978), Jim Jefferies (1977),
Rob Thomas (1972), Simon Pegg (1970), Michael Bloomberg
(1942)

15th February

Gary Clark Jr. (1984), Alex Borstein (1971), Shepard Fairey
(1970), Chris Farley (1964), Matt Groening (1954), Janice
Dickinson (1955), Jane Seymour (1951), Irena Sendler (1874),
Susan B. Anthony (1820)

16th February

The Weeknd (1990), Elizabeth Olsen (1989), Valentino
Rossi (1979), Philipp Plein (1978), Amanda Holden (1971),
Christopher Eccleston (1964), John McEnroe (1959), Ice-T
(1958), Eckhart Tolle (1948)

17th February

Marc Márquez (1993), Ed Sheeran (1991), Bonnie Wright
(1991), Joseph Gordon-Levitt (1981), Paris Hilton (1981),
Billie Joe Armstrong (1972), Denise Richards (1971), Michael
Jordan (1963), Rene Russo (1954)

18th February

Le'Veon Bell (1992), Jeremy Allen White (1991), Jillian Michaels (1974), Molly Ringwald (1968), Matt Dillon (1964), John Travolta (1954), Cybill Shepherd (1950), Paco Rabanne (1934), Yoko Ono (1933), Toni Morrison (1931), Enzo Ferrari (1898)

19th February

Mauro Icardi (1993), Victoria Justice (1993), Arielle Kebbel (1985), David Gandy (1980), Seal (1963), Benicio del Toro (1957), Jeff Daniels (1955), Tony Iommi (1948), Cristina Fernández de Kirchner, Argentinian President (1953)

CONTENTS
....